BASEBALL ON THE PRAIRIE

HOW SEVEN SMALL-TOWN TEAMS SHAPED TEXAS LEAGUE HISTORY

KRIS RUTHERFORD

FOREWORD BY SCOTT HANZELKA

THE History PRESS

Published by The History Press
Charleston, SC 29403
www.historypress.net

First published 2014

Manufactured in the United States

ISBN 978.1.60949.935.8

Library of Congress CIP data applied for.

To Mom and Dad, for whom small-town North Texas will always be home.

CONTENTS

FOREWORD

The Texas League has a long and storied history, sparking my interest in both the league and the sport of baseball in general. I have been researching the Texas League for over thirty years and have had the great fortune of assisting in editing the *Texas League Media Guide and Record Book* for the past twenty. During this time, I have read many fine books on the Texas League to aid in my research, but the one area not well documented is the smaller cities of the early league. If not for growing cities such as Sherman, Denison, Paris, Corsicana, Texarkana and Cleburne, the league may have not survived the late 1890s and early 1900s.

The Texas League began as Texas was growing in population and becoming stronger economically due to ranching and the discovery of oil. The lure of riches led the railroad industry in expanding, and Texas communities soon realized the railroad offered opportunities for growth in business and population.

Cities such as Sherman, Denison and Paris began looking for ways to prove they had arrived as up-and-coming commercial centers. One way to do so was to attract a professional baseball team in the fledgling Texas League. These communities saw the Texas League as a way to prove to their citizens that they were ready to compete with the larger cities of Dallas, Fort Worth, Galveston and San Antonio. The Texas League saw the smaller cities as bridges between the northern and southern divisions of the league. The railroads also saw this opportunity and often worked out deals for player transport. In many cases, they provided land for a team's ballpark. It is interesting to note that parks were often located at the end of a rail line or near a prominent stop.

The combination of these factors creates an interesting part of Texas League history. The smaller cities, much like their larger counterparts, had their ups and downs, ranging from the 1897 Paris Texas Midlands 41-80 record and the 1902 Corsicana Oil City Indians 87-23 season. Kris Rutherford skillfully blends the historical aspects of each community with the history of the early Texas League, making what follows an interesting read for history and baseball fans alike.

Scott Hanzelka

ACKNOWLEDGEMENTS

This book could not have been completed without the assistance of several individuals and organizations. First and foremost, I thank my traveling companion, photographer and wife, Karen, for her patience throughout this process, as well as my research assistant and youngest son, Kolton. Early Texas League history is interesting. In one day, we might have found ourselves in the library of Austin College in Sherman, along the abandoned tracks of the Texas and Pacific Railroad and wandering around what is left of Grayson County's tiny community of Tom Bean. Our searches of North Texas cemeteries, many lost in the brush along narrow dirt roads, for the graves of forgotten Texas Leaguers was a fascinating experience, as was our quest to discover the sites of ballparks often abandoned for a century.

I also thank Texas League president Tom Kayser for his advice and direction. The Lamar County Historical Society, the Grayson County Historical Society and Sherman Museum, the Ennis Railroad and Cultural Museum, the Ennis Chamber of Commerce and the Clara Foster Slough Museum in Enloe all provided additional assistance. Likewise, Bobby Young and the Navarro County Historical Society, Mary Ann Hicks, Butch Garrison, the University of North Texas, AntiqueMystique.com, Greenville Revisited, Grayson County GenWeb, the Bell County historical website (txbell.net), Save Old Cleburne, Ron Maxfield, Robin Johnson and numerous anonymous citizens throughout North Texas pointed me in the right direction when needed.

I wish to give special thanks to Fred Finlayson and Mary Ann Thebo Finlayson of Idaho Falls, Idaho, and the late Guy S. Rall III of Houston, Texas, for their invaluable assistance in obtaining family history related to their ancestors who participated in the early Texas League. Mrs. Thebo's uncle, Tony, initially piqued my interest in the subject, and without her assistance, this book would have focused far more on box scores than old-time baseball's most important legacy—the personalities who made the game.

Finally, I offer an enormous debt of gratitude to Texas League aficionado Scott Hanzelka. This book would not have been possible without Scott's tenacious and meticulous research of early Texas newspapers in search of box scores, game descriptions, statistics and chronological information. His research is used annually in developing the *Texas League Media Guide*, and I know of no greater authority on the league's early history. Scott offered advice and information throughout the course of my research, available to seek out even the most minute detail upon request.

PROLOGUE

Tony Thebo is perhaps Paris's most unheralded ballplayer. George, Tony's father, introduced the young Texas city to baseball soon after the Civil War. When the younger Thebo grew into a teenager, he wowed the hometown crowd as an amateur ballplayer. Mentored by fellow Parisian Ben Shelton, Tony became the fastest base runner in Paris. A hawk in the outfield, Tony turned sure extra-base hits into routine fly balls and gunned down would-be runs at the plate from seemingly anywhere on the field. He never forgot his roots or the people who helped him enjoy a long minor-league career.

George Thebo encouraged Tony to learn the game of baseball, and without his enthusiasm, Tony would probably never have graced a baseball diamond. Tony's mother expressed unquestioned disgust at baseball and ballplayers in general, but George offered his son silent encouragement in the face of his wife's disapproval. In 1900, when Tony and his younger brother Willie watched their father's casket lowered into a grave in Paris's Evergreen Cemetery, Tony recalled his support as he prepared for his professional career.

Throughout Tony's career, he saw a few Texas League colleagues meet untimely deaths. Teammate and league pioneer "Big" Mike O'Connor succumbed to tuberculosis before the 1906 season, his death shocking the entire league. After players and executives from across the state gathered in Austin in his honor, some may have forgotten Big Mike's contribution to the Texas League, a baseball circuit that may not have survived the 1890s

Karen Rutherford photo.

Karen Rutherford photo.

without his support. Six years later, when former teammate Rube Taylor took a fateful step in front of a Dallas streetcar, few recalled the one-time major leaguer's ties to Texas League baseball. Still, Tony remembered both of the old ballplayers' contributions.

Tony never played aside Walt "Hickory" Dickson, but he did face the tenacious hurler's overpowering fastball. When Dickson succumbed to the flu in 1918, a few former teammates gathered for his funeral in Greenville, and a few more sent flowers. Some recalled Dickson as the pitcher who never fulfilled his potential, his magnificent 1906 season a distant memory. Tony, though, remembered what Dickson could have been.

Tony Thebo never appeared in the big leagues. His fast glove, powerful arm and speed on the base paths made him a force to be reckoned with at the minor-league level, but his light bat drew little interest from major-league teams playing in the Deadball Era. To the contrary, good friend Ben Shelton found himself in demand. After a few minor-league seasons in the northern states, Shelton returned to Texas with a refined game and represented a legitimate threat at the plate. But unlike so many other ballplayers of his day, Shelton had no interest in leaving Texas, and major-league scouts soon forgot his talent. Tony watched, learned and vowed to remember.

As the nation entered the Roaring Twenties, the Texas League grew from a fledgling circuit of castoffs to a major source of big-league talent. Yet many

Karen Rutherford photo.

Karen Rutherford photo.

of the league's early pioneers died off with little fanfare. In 1929, throngs of friends and admirers laid longtime league president J. Doak Roberts to rest beneath a sprawling tree in Corsicana's Oakwood Cemetery. Soon, few strolling through the cemetery would take notice of Roberts's modest headstone or consider his importance in the development of the Texas League. Tony remembered.

Though Tony mourned the passing of many of the Texas League's finest over the next few decades, mortality didn't truly hit home until 1945, when Ben Shelton died in Terrell. When the Texas Midland Railroad carried Shelton's body home to Paris, Tony accompanied his longtime friend to his final resting place. As Tony stood aside Ben's freshly dug grave and spotted his father's headstone in the distance, he knew most Texas baseball fans had already forgotten his friend's contribution to their favorite sport, but Tony kept his vow. He remembered.

A few of Tony's baseball acquaintances, like Hunter Hill, Charley Moran and Otto McIvor, lived until the 1950s and met occasionally to remember the old days. By mid-century, though, the Old Timer reunions came to an end as the number of surviving players grew small. For Tony, the memories remained vivid, and fellow Temple resident Roy Mitchell's death in 1959 served to remind him he was among the few left to pass along Texas baseball's earliest history.

By 1960, Tony Thebo had grown into an old man for his day. Tony and Anne, his wife of a half century, lived quietly in Temple, never having had children. Baseball had become an obsession not even the most rabid 1890s ballplayer could have dreamed. Live radio and television broadcasts, larger-than-life heroes and the annual World Series transformed professional baseball from small, loosely organized leagues into a major industry. Even the Texas League, once an oft-changing group of franchises simply trying to hold together for an entire summer, had become a core of major-league talent, sending a steady stream of young players to their big-league affiliates.

Tony Thebo's friends and neighbors probably had a sense of the history of the old man living at 715 West Garland Avenue. Perhaps they knew he was a light-hitting outfielder who didn't quite make the big leagues but still held Texas League records for base running. They may have heard the story of the time Tony started a brawl in a Paris semipro game when the umpire's companions objected to his questioning their friend's eyesight. Some may have even heard him speak with pride of his little brother Willie's brief professional career in the Arkansas State League. But those Tony remembered so vividly had mostly passed into history. Mike O'Connor hadn't been mentioned in a newspaper in half a century. Ben Shelton lay in a Paris grave marked with a simple headstone and no sign he ever graced a baseball field. Doak Roberts rested only an hour or so northeast of Temple, but few passing by his grave realized his ties to Hall of Fame outfielder Tris Speaker, whose grave lay just a few miles north. Still, even as he approached eighty years of age, Tony Thebo remembered them all.

Tony and Anne Thebo enthusiastically greeted the arrival of 1966. Just a few months earlier, Tony had celebrated his eighty-fourth birthday. With few close relatives, Tony and Anne had spent the holidays quietly enjoying one another's company and greeting the visitors who stopped by to see the elderly couple at their Temple home. The coming year promised more of the same quiet life, but Anne's mere presence and the weekly Saturday afternoon baseball broadcast on NBC kept Tony more than satisfied. He looked forward to the newspaper reports from spring training and fully intended to follow the major leagues all the way through the October Classic.

January 5, 1966, dawned cool and cloudy in Temple. Tony planned an afternoon of yard work ahead of the rain forecast for the next couple days. Still spry in his mid-eighties, the exercise would do him well, and after another of Anne's fine home-cooked meals, Tony headed to the front yard and began raking leaves. An hour later, Anne came to check his progress. She found Tony motionless, facedown atop his rake. One of the few remaining Texas League baseball players of the early twentieth century, Anthony Valle Thebo was dead of a heart attack.

In the coming days, a few news reports recognized Tony's passing. Newspapers in Amarillo, Abilene and San Antonio mentioned Tony's death in two-sentence articles buried in the sports sections, while the *Paris News* provided two- or three-inch columns briefly covering the long-forgotten hometown hero's accomplishments. The *Dallas Morning News*, among the most trusted sources of information regarding the Texas League since its founding in 1888, offered no mention of Thebo's death.

A few days after he died, Anne Thebo laid Tony to rest in her family plot at the rear of Temple's Hillcrest Cemetery. The couple's friends attended the service, but the old ballplayer had few relatives and even fewer baseball colleagues left. To his last day, though, Tony kept his vow to George Thebo and the many players who had passed before him. He remembered. Now, with a half-century's worth of Tony's memories packed away, Anne was left to keep them alive.

Following Tony's funeral, Anne chose a twelve-inch by eighteen-inch marker matching the rest of those in the family plot, inscribed simply "A.V.

Karen Rutherford photo.

Thebo, Sept. 1, 1881–Jan. 5, 1966." As many widows did, she placed a marker atop her own future grave with her name and birth date inscribed but the date of death left blank. For the rest of her life, Anne passed Tony's baseball memories along to those who would listen, frequently recalling his many stories and legends. Finally, on February 7, 1981, Anne Thebo died at the age of ninety-five. With virtually no living relatives and most friends already gone, few noticed her passing, and even fewer attended the graveside service in which she was buried next to Tony. Some thirty years later, the two markers remain side by side, but no one inscribed Anne's date of death on her stone. Anne kept Tony's memories alive for fifteen years after his death. When she passed, there was no one left to remember.

CHAPTER 1

TEXAS: NO LEISURE ON THE NEW FRONTIER

Pioneers migrating to North Texas in the late 1830s hadn't heard of baseball; in fact, neither had most Americans. People in the Northeast played a primitive form of the sport known as "town ball" or "round ball"; however, the rules varied from place to place, and most considered the game little more than a passing fad. After all, leisure time remained elusive in nineteenth-century America. The thought of wasting precious spare time on a game seemed unthinkable to most. For those moving to the new Republic of Texas, on the other hand, spare time simply didn't exist.

While some saw hope and opportunity on the western frontier, most Americans placed their faith in the Industrial Revolution. Just a generation earlier, the War of 1812 revealed the country's flawed manufacturing and transportation systems, and industrial advancement had since spread rapidly. Eli Whitney's 1793 cotton gin offered an early glimpse of technology's potential, and by the first half of the nineteenth century, this simple invention sparked frenzied economic growth. Southern cotton plantations provided northern textile mills raw material for mass production, and the seemingly limitless crop increased demand for cotton-based goods, a supply-and-demand chain bringing tremendous advancement in manufacturing technologies. As the cotton industry grew, engineers adapted textile technologies to other industries, and manufacturing grew exponentially.

The economic health of the new industrial sector required an efficient distribution system. In the early 1800s, transportation infrastructure like the Erie Canal cut shipping time and cost, but industrial leaders recognized the nation's economic future when the first stretch of railroad opened between Baltimore and Frederick, Maryland. The railroad age arriving, by 1831, America stood on the cusp of a major societal shift. Manufacturing would soon be just as important as agriculture, and the diversity would improve all aspects of life. Americans looked forward to a mobile society and quality, reasonably priced goods made by skilled workers who commanded higher wages and shorter workweeks. Still, the farther west one traveled, the less one felt the Industrial Revolution's impact. Socioeconomic change turned much slower than the wagon wheels headed for Texas.

Americans enjoyed leisure activities like theater and dancing long before the Revolutionary War, and as the nineteenth century neared its midpoint, they demanded even more amusements. City planners set aside green spaces for parks, and activities like kite flying, festivals and outdoor games grew popular. In time, town ball became more organized, and standardized rules helped the game grow. Other sporting competitions like boxing, horse racing and cockfighting attracted both spectators and gamblers. Increased disposable income meant people were willing to pay for entertainment, and recreation in the eastern United States commercialized. On the other hand, no elaborate opera houses, manicured parks or grand ballrooms operated on the prairies of North Texas. A wild frontier greeted settlers, with nothing except backbreaking hard work to tame it. Even hunting, a sport for many back east, became a basic means of survival on the new frontier.

While their new home offered few comforts, most early Texans already hailed from undeveloped areas of the country. Many migrated from farms in Kentucky and Tennessee, while others arrived from the rural Midwest. Still, as the pioneers crossed the Red River or traveled northward from Galveston, they found a land nothing like that they left behind. A tall-grass prairie rooted in black soil as fertile as any in the United States covered North Texas. The blackland prairie could have easily supported a lucrative cotton industry, but few settlers owned slaves, leaving them to grow less labor-intensive crops like corn and wheat. Regardless, the new Texans did not lack optimism. The Red River and its tributaries provided plenty of water. Wildlife like buffalo, white-tailed deer, bobcats, quail and other commercially valuable species filled the prairies. Settlers found timber along creek banks and in the "Big Thickets" breaking up the prairie. Many found local Indians eager to trade. The settlers marveled at the vast resources Texas offered.

Texas's seemingly unlimited potential did not come without peril. Fires in the tall-grass prairie devastated families. Indian tribes like the Wichita grew hostile toward the invaders of their sacred territory. The oppressively hot summers overwhelmed even those accustomed to a southern climate, and crops withered in periods of drought. Early North Texans faced many of the same challenges as those in pre-colonial New England, with climate, Native Americans and ignorance of local agricultural methods detrimental to daily life. Still, new Texans arrived regularly. Soon the trickle of pioneers became a steady flow.

As North Texas grew, small communities formed. People with common heritage banded together in settlements like Kentuckytown in Grayson County, while others congregated around transportation routes like the Trinity River at present-day Dallas. Most communities, though, developed out of socioeconomic need. People met in central locations to share ideas and obtain the few goods available for survival. Before long, stores and trading posts emerged, and settlers built homesteads nearby. Economies grew around these new communities, and they became important centers of politics, commerce and social growth.

Soon, the harsh realities of the frontier began to ease. By statehood in 1845, treaties with Native Americans reduced threats of attack, and tribes moved to reservations or across the Red River into present-day Oklahoma. Intense farming broke the prairie's dense sod, and land routes from Galveston and Jefferson brought wagons and a steady supply of dry goods. Mercantile businesses attracted saloons and brothels as enterprising individuals sought to provide diversions for local residents and travelers. These establishments represented a culture later romanticized in novels, movies and music and provided Americans a vision of Texas as a rugged, lawless frontier. More importantly, though, they represented the first commercial recreation ventures in North Texas.

Those who clung to the Puritan values and religious convictions of the Northeast likened Texas's limited recreation opportunities to the work of the devil. Promoting idleness and detracting from the work ethic, many considered the gambling, prostitution and drunkenness in their growing communities morally reprehensible. Even as more acceptable forms of recreation arrived, some settlers resisted the leisure pursuits shaping Texas culture. Most, though, took little notice and continued to carve out an agriculture-based frontier life. Only an enterprising few saw the growth of recreation for what it truly represented—opportunity.

CHAPTER 2

THE CIVIL WAR, RECONSTRUCTION AND BASEBALL: DIVISION AND DIVERSION

Suddenly there was a scattering of fire, [of] *which three outfielders caught the brunt; the center field was hit and was captured, left and right field managed to get back to our lines. The attack...was repelled without serious difficulty, but we had lost not only our centerfield, but...the only baseball in Alexandria.*
—George A. Putnam, Union soldier

The first baseball game in Texas remains undocumented. George Putnam's account of his Civil War experience near Alexandria, Louisiana, took place well east of the Texas border, but his passage supports what many believe—that Union soldiers largely introduced modern baseball to the South during the Civil War. While some Rebel soldiers from port cities had learned portions of the game from northern seamen before the war, most of the Confederate exposure to baseball came from watching their enemies play the game in encampments and inside prisoner of war camps. Diaries of Union prisoners at Camp Ford near Tyler speak of baseball being played in the camp, with the soldiers forming a ball from a piece of cork wound in blanket thread and covered in leather. The Rebel guards must have been intrigued at the competitive spirit the contests brought out in their prisoners' otherwise bleak lives. Even though crude forms of the game had been played in the South for some time, the Rebels marveled at the northern game's refined rules and skilled positioning of players.

Some of the same guards from Camp Ford may have participated in Texas's first recorded baseball game on April 21, 1867. The Houston Stonewalls celebrated the anniversary of Texas's independence from Mexico by defeating the Galveston Robert E. Lee's 35–2 on the San Jacinto battlefield. Regardless of when or how the game arrived in the state, however, it is clear that soon after the Civil War, the same "base ball" fever sweeping the nation arrived in Texas.

The northern tier of Texas counties voted against secession leading up to the war, but when hostilities began, most men broke ranks with the popular vote and joined the Confederate cause. Charles William Batsell, a twenty-two-year-old Grayson County resident whose father owned just one of the county's two hundred slaves, enlisted in the Sixteenth Texas Cavalry under Fitzhugh's command. After mustering at Clarksville, his company soon stationed at Little Rock, Arkansas, and saw its first combat at the Battle of Cotton Plant along the White River. When Rebel commanders ordered the cavalry dismounted, Batsell joined "Walker's Greyhounds," an infantry division nicknamed for its ability to march long distances on short notice. Batsell and his unit crisscrossed southern Arkansas and Louisiana for nearly three years, taking part in the Vicksburg and Red River Campaigns and the Camden Expedition. With Union troops scattered throughout both Arkansas and Louisiana and combat sporadic, it is likely that Batsell witnessed baseball being played during raids like those described by George Putnam. Whether or not Southerners attempted to mimic the game in their own camps remains unknown.

Will Batsell held little interest in the rural lifestyle. An enterprising young man, he saw a future in goods and services and, while assigned to the Confederate Commissary, gained valuable experience in inventory and distribution channels. Returning to North Texas after the war, Batsell spent two years as postmaster in Kentuckytown before moving to Sherman, the fledgling county seat a dozen miles northwest. Will Batsell found Sherman a ramshackle town suffering the same economic hardships plaguing the rest of the South. With supplies limited and their Confederate money now worthless, local residents faced a bleak future as Reconstruction began. Will, on the other hand, clung to a positive vision.

With the states once again united, the technology and transportation systems of the Northeast slowly made their way to Texas. Texans looked forward to railroad and manufacturing jobs, reduced work hours and more leisure time. As the country closed its most turbulent decade, Will Batsell foresaw a prosperous Sherman steeped in commerce and culture, with recreation and transportation fueling both.

While Will Batsell's unit patrolled the western theater, Leonidas Linville Maughs engaged in some of the Civil War's fiercest fighting in

Tennessee and Georgia. Rebellion ran in Maughs's bloodlines. The son of a Missouri physician who owned six slaves, Maughs's family lineage dated to seventeenth-century Virginia, and several of his ancestors fought for the Continental army during the American Revolution. With the onset of the Civil War, Maughs, a store clerk in his Missouri hometown, quickly joined the Rebel cause, enlisting in Captain Hiram Bledsoe's Missouri Battery. He first saw action at Fort Pillow, Carthage, Wilson's Creek and Pea Ridge west of the Mississippi but moved to Chattanooga by late 1863. Maughs fought at the Battle of Chickamauga, where some news accounts credited him with killing Union general and Civil War poet William Haines Lytle. Despite his act of valor, Maughs probably didn't feel a sense of achievement, as even his fellow Rebel soldiers mourned the death of the well-known general, placing a wreath over his body and reciting his poetry in his honor.

As the war drew to a close, Maughs remained in Georgia, eventually wounded and taken prisoner at the Battle of West Point. Transferred to Nashville with other prisoners, the Confederate surrender at Appomattox hastened his released after only two weeks. Assigned the rank of major upon discharge, admirers referred to him as "Major Maughs" for the remainder of his life.

Unlike Batsell, Leonidas Maughs did not return home at war's end. Instead, he became a lawyer in Corinth, Mississippi, just a few miles south of Shiloh, the site of one of the war's bloodiest battles. By 1876, he relocated to the young railroad town of Denison, Texas, where he served as superintendent of the local gaslight company, as well as a lawyer and postmaster. Major Maughs represented Denison in a number of capacities and took great interest in the future of his adopted city. Like Will Batsell, Maughs recognized the growing demand for leisure and recreation. By 1890, he helped found the Denison Rod and Gun Club, was named its first president and traveled with fellow members into newly settled Oklahoma on quail hunts. Likewise, he took great interest in the amateur baseball games regularly played in Forest Park, contests often pitting Denison against Sherman, its neighbor just nine miles south.

Honey Grove and Bonham. Commerce and Wolfe City. Petty and Roxton.

None of these North Texas towns are known for baseball, but at one time, each boasted its own traveling "Nine" town ball club. Although not the original town ball played in the Northeast before the Civil War, the

Above: A game of town ball played in Brookston (Lamar County), circa 1910. *Courtesy of Phillip Rutherford.*

Opposite: Early Enloe (Delta County) uniform typical of those worn by town ball teams. *Karen Rutherford photo.*

ENLOE

modified game proved a highly popular form of local entertainment. Entire communities often turned out for a town ball game, the players dressed in elaborate uniforms any major leaguer would wear with pride. A rough bare lot or pasture on the outskirts of town fit the bill as a ball field, most often ending in a high-scoring, error-filled game. Still, rivalries became intense as each community supported its homegrown talent. Animosity between communities grew as players, coaches, umpires and "rooters" frequently brawled after disputed plays. A team tiring of its competition might place an announcement in the newspaper seeking new opponents, sometimes publicly challenging a specific community to a ballgame. More often than not, the challenged team accepted, setting off a war of words filling newspapers for a week. The games seldom lived up to their billing, and the newspaper editors who hyped them most often buried the results in a single sentence between advertisements for manly footwear or medicinal concoctions.

Despite the allure of town ball, visiting teams almost always played at a disadvantage. Transportation via horses, mules and wagons made travel to even nearby towns time consuming, and the heat, rough ride, thirst and hunger might defeat a team before it even arrived at the ball field. Rosters shifted depending on how much work lay in the fields, no organized schedules existed, teams split gate receipts (if any) without accounting and rules seemingly changed mid-game. A man willing to serve as umpire placed his life in the hands of a crowd easily turned hostile and offered rulings in favor of the home team as much out of fear as fairness. A shellacking on a dusty diamond often added humiliation, and players might return home vowing to never play the game again. But baseball held a seemingly universal allure. Many small towns clung to their teams for decades, sometimes fielding two or even three teams if local talent warranted. Still, with few exceptions, these town ball teams normally stayed close to home and local competition. In the mid-1870s, though, the railroad's arrival changed baseball in the Lone Star State forever.

Early Texas settlers relied on primitive transportation. Steamboats only navigated rivers near the coastal region, although they could access as far inland as the port of Jefferson via the Red River from Louisiana. In time, the Red River provided easy transportation to North Texas, but until then, the Great Raft, a centuries-old dam of driftwood, fallen trees and other debris, formed a blockade to all navigation north of present-day Shreveport.

So with waterway travel limited, most transportation relied on mule and oxen power. This inherently inefficient, expensive and unreliable shipping method lay at the mercy of weather that often made crude wagon trails muddy and impassable.

The Texas Congress authorized construction of a railroad within months of winning independence from Mexico, but it wasn't until 1851 that the state's first line began to take shape. Spearheaded by General Sidney Sherman, the Buffalo Bayou, Brazos and Colorado Railroad opened a twenty-mile line between Harrisburg and Stafford two years later. By 1856, the Galveston and Red River Railway opened its own twenty-five-mile route in the Houston area and soon changed its name to the Houston and Texas Central (HTC), with plans to lay track all the way to the Red River in Grayson County. By the outset of the Civil War, Texas boasted nearly five hundred miles of rail line, most of it in the populated southeast coastal area.

The Civil War brought most railroad construction to a halt, and with materials in short supply, existing rail fell into disrepair. Railroad companies took some lines out of service for the war's duration, but construction and repairs resumed after the South surrendered. The HTC led the way, continuing northward and reaching Corsicana by 1871. Two years later, the railroad completed its run through Dallas to the Red River nearly two decades after initial construction began. New railroads soon connected Houston, San Antonio and Austin. Meanwhile, the Texas and Pacific Railroad, a southern transcontinental route, stretched a line from Texarkana to Dallas/Fort Worth via Tyler, as well as a northern route from Sherman across Fannin County toward Texarkana. The Missouri, Kansas and Texas, historically known as "the Katy," crossed into Grayson County from the Red River, and the Cotton Belt line stretched through east-central and north Texas. By the late 1880s, railroads connected all of the state's major cities. Small communities along the routes prospered. In many cases, the railroad itself formed communities at junctions, machine yards and switch stations. Corsicana, Temple, Denison, Cleburne and Terrell all owed their existences to the railroads, and the industry employed most of each community's citizens. For some Texas settlements, though, the arrival of the railroad signaled their demise. Surveyors planned routes based on finances, topography, land values and potential for development. Aside from county seats, rail companies seldom changed course to serve a specific town. Experience had proven that populations naturally migrated to the railroad right of way. Bypassed communities either disappeared or lost status as they came to rely on the newly founded towns along the line for goods and services.

The railroad gave rise to manufacturing jobs and an industrial culture. Railroad employees associated with a "brand" and began to identify with their employers. Executives understood satisfied employees as less likely to unionize and more likely to exhibit loyalty. Railroad companies wanted a community presence, particularly in towns like Sherman and Denison, where multiple lines fought for business. Employees served as ambassadors for their companies, encouraging local support and advertising their hometowns along the railroad route.

Widespread industrial baseball didn't arrive until World War I, but several Texas railroads sponsored one or more employee baseball teams in the late nineteenth century to offer entertainment for workers, their families and the community. In some cases, a railroad might recruit a professional ballplayer or two—paid rail hands during the week who earned even more money playing ball on weekends. Railroad teams often played other business-sponsored clubs like those from post offices, cotton gins and drugstores. If no other opponent could be found, a railroad might form its own league, with the business office, yard workers, locomotive mechanics and rail maintenance departments fighting for company supremacy. For employees, though, contests between competing railroads like the Katy and Cotton Belt drew the most interest. When railroad teams played baseball, the on-field outcome, at least in perception, signaled business success. Newspaper coverage represented free advertising, and some rail executives believed the winning team gained an upper hand on the opposing company. After all, everyone wanted to ride on a winner.

The railroads brought much more than efficient transportation to Texas. Samuel Morse's telegraph, invented in the 1830s, revolutionized railroad communications. Though Texas's first telegraph office in Marshall connected to Shreveport, New Orleans and Natchez through wires strung in trees, telegraph lines soon followed railroad right of ways. Railroads and telegraph lines accompanied each other, and modern communication soon reached all communities along a rail route. The famed tycoon Jay Gould, operator of several railroads in Texas, also owned Western Union, the largest telegraph company in the United States. Gould installed telegraph lines along his rails to serve his company and generate a secondary source of income. Western Union offices popped up all over Texas, and the public could soon transmit private messages for a fee. By 1870, over 1,500 miles of telegraph lines crossed the state, connecting all major cities.

Efficient communication bolstered interest in baseball. Local teams issued challenges via telegraph rather than newspaper and could schedule a contest within a day's time. Reporters transmitted scores and other baseball news to their papers daily, with games played just hours earlier headlining the sports page the next morning. Daily standings, statistics and play-by-play accounts of each game drew great interest, increasing newspaper circulation and encouraging even more coverage. By 1885, the *Galveston News* established Texas's first official news wire, transmitting information throughout the state and beyond. Texas baseball news soon filled newsstands throughout the country.

Railroads connected cities, but within a community, the horse and carriage remained the common means of travel. As towns grew, so did demand for public transportation. Initially, entrepreneurs brought a scaled-down stagecoach system to the cities, but these taxis fell subject to the elements and were easily bogged down in mud-filled streets. Innovative businessmen looked to long-distance railroads for solutions, and soon steel rails stretched along major thoroughfares. Mules easily pulled streetcars along the rails, allowing for larger vehicles carrying more passengers. Local traction companies soon operated in most North Texas cities.

Baseball and the railroad rolled on parallel tracks, the railroad's rapid expansion after the Civil War coinciding with baseball's growing popularity. The first professional teams formed in the late 1860s, traveling throughout the northern states and challenging local teams, a form of scheduling known as "barnstorming." Even amateur teams now traveled significant distances, stirring up rivalries between communities far apart on the map. Just as importantly, the railroads offered affordable fares allowing local spectators to travel along with their teams. Fewer partisan crowds meant fewer intimidated umpires, fair play and improved community relations. Teams from the northern states soon barnstormed Texas as well, setting up pre-season competitions statewide. As the railroad system continued to grow, small communities grew larger, economies improved and citizens found free time and money on their hands. While some continued to protest the immoral nature of sport in general (and gambling was no stranger to the grandstands), baseball held a firm grip on society. Ladies even attended baseball games, taking advantage of the free admission promotions many teams offered.

Texas railroads found baseball good for business. Ball clubs traveled exclusively by rail, and most negotiated transportation contracts before the season. Based on a common rate of two cents per mile per player, a team of ten traveled from Denison to Austin for about fifty dollars. To reduce travel costs, league officials organized northern and southern swings for each team, allowing a northern team to visit all southern cities on a single trip and vice versa. Railroads discounted rates for fan excursions, sometimes carrying spectators between cities for as low as one dollar per round trip. The most rabid fan could travel the longest road trip in the Texas League, Sherman to Galveston, for nine dollars. Locally, mule-powered streetcar companies financed ballparks on the outskirts of town, essentially forcing spectators without other transportation to travel by streetcar to catch a game. Baseball franchises profited by not having to invest in a ballpark, and local transport services increased patronage.

Like transportation companies, many other businesses profited from baseball. Local merchants stocked sporting equipment, and businesses closed early on game days. Texans eagerly anticipated baseball season, and newspapers reported both on- and off-field happenings in the sport on a local and national level. Baseball grew into a form of commerce, and businessmen in every community searched for a way to gain a foothold.

CHAPTER 3

PROFESSIONAL BASEBALL: FAITH AND FAILURE IN TEXAS

When baseball pioneer John McCloskey met with prospective team owners in 1887 to develop a Texas circuit, he expected the sport to be a rousing success. Since the railroads arrived in the 1870s, northern professional teams barnstorming the state played before large, enthusiastic crowds. McCloskey himself played a number of games in Texas as an amateur and brought his Joplin Independents on a tour in the fall of 1887. He marveled at the turnout in Austin, Fort Worth and Waco. The Southern League of the southeastern states had proven a market for baseball existed outside the Northeast, and Texas seemed a natural place to expand the national game.

At McCloskey's urging, representatives of the largest Texas cities of Austin, Dallas, Houston, Fort Worth, Galveston, San Antonio and Waco, as well as New Orleans, Louisiana, turned out for a December 1887 meeting in Austin. A month later, a second meeting resulted in a six-team league. With franchises awarded to San Antonio, Austin, Dallas, Fort Worth, Houston and Galveston, officials planned an overly ambitious April–October schedule. The first team to struggle financially, San Antonio folded in late May. Several weeks later, the Austin franchise relocated to the Alamo City, and the New Orleans Pelicans joined the circuit. Any sense of stability lasted only a few weeks as Houston and Galveston soon ceased operations. By September 2, only three teams remained in Texas's first professional baseball league, and the 1888 season drew to a close a month early when New Orleans elected to forgo another road trip to Texas. Dallas claimed the championship with the best overall record.

WORTH

Dallas's Oriental Hotel (above) and Fort Worth's Worth Hotel (left) hosted many meetings of Texas League pioneers. *Author's collection.*

McCloskey found the initial Texas League season a disappointment, but the novelty of professional baseball held over to 1889, when Waco joined the league along with Dallas, Fort Worth, Austin, Houston and Galveston. Despite success on the field, McCloskey's Houston team folded in early August, joined by Austin. The entire league followed suit a few days later, with third-place Austin crowned as disputed champion until Houston paid its league dues. Though falling short of completing a full schedule, the 1889 Texas League remained intact from start to finish. No teams relocated, a positive sign in an era when baseball clubs frequently changed cities on a moment's notice.

Officials organized a third attempt at a league in 1890, but by early June, three of the six franchises dropped out, and the league dissolved. With the Texas League's first three seasons unprofitable, officials could not find financial backing for a fourth. No one attempted to reorganize the league for 1891.

In 1892, John McCloskey returned to Texas and assembled a four-team league of Dallas, Fort Worth, Houston and Galveston. Eager to expand the small circuit, McCloskey continued to lobby additional backers as the season played out, and when both Fort Worth and Dallas disbanded in June, San Antonio and Waco quickly replaced them. Representatives of Sherman lobbied for a spot in the league as well, but McCloskey committed only to the largest cities and gave little consideration to the community only seventy-five miles north of Dallas. Despite his plan, fan support in McCloskey's chosen cities could not hold up a full six months, and the 1892 season ended nearly two months ahead of schedule.

Even the most optimistic supporters regarded the first few years of Texas professional baseball as failures. In an effort to gain an upper hand on the competition, owners failed to follow self-imposed salary caps, creating financial instability. The league also drew a comparatively lowly class of ballplayer, known for poor performance both on and off the field. Players drank heavily and patronized brothels, embarrassing both themselves and team owners. Attendance suffered. At twenty-five cents a ticket, people preferred to pocket their money rather than spend it to support poor play and unruly ballplayers. Following the failed 1892 season, no one made efforts to continue the league in 1893 or 1894.

Although Texas had no organized professional baseball circuit for two full seasons, promoters continued to see the state as a potential hotbed for the sport. In early 1894, the *Sporting News* reported an expected "grand revival of baseball in Texas next year," as there was "no decent ball" in the area.

John McCloskey, founder of the Texas League. *Author's collection.*

The *News* noted the state's geographic advantages, with an equal number of large northern and southern cities situated at reasonable intervals allowing daily play. Likewise, all major cities allowed Sunday baseball, a luxury many of the second-tier cities did not offer. The *News* emphasized success relying on owners adhering to a strict salary cap and bringing in top ballplayers, a marked change from their previous willingness to settle for castoffs of more successful leagues.

The *Dallas Morning News* agreed with writers of the *Sporting News*, noting that if the owners didn't let their "pocketbooks run away with their judgment," a permanent league was possible. "Baseball has a firm grip on the west," it noted, and recent years had seen the price of players cut in half.

By February 1894, Austin baseball supporters encouraged Mike O'Connor, a Texan playing ball in St. Joseph, Missouri, to organize a Texas circuit. Although captaining a team of several players with Texas ties, O'Connor balked, noting that the state was not yet ready for "good ball," but conceded he would be willing to try again in 1895. By May, however, St. Joseph manager Joe Nolan committed to barnstorming Texas after its season with games planned in Denison, Sherman, Corsicana, Fort Worth, Waco, Austin, San Antonio, Houston and Galveston. Though likely chosen only because they were situated along the rail line, Nolan's inclusion of Denison, Sherman and Corsicana offered opportunities for the smaller communities to showcase their own enthusiasm for quality baseball.

As McCloskey had realized a few years earlier, Texas's geography offered great benefit in reducing transportation costs. Railroads served Houston and Galveston, San Antonio and Austin and Dallas and Fort Worth, and the relatively short distance between each couplet of cities allowed teams to play several games while accumulating limited travel expenses. League discussions involving adding or removing cities from the circuit always boiled down to "the jump"—the distance and associated cost of traveling from one city to another. Owners worked feverishly to ensure jumps remained short and economical, often passing on distant cities otherwise able to support a team. Some cities' officials offered guaranteed gate receipts or arranged discounted rail fares for the opportunity to host a franchise, but more often than not, these efforts failed. Baseball's success depended on financing, and a compact, geographically balanced league ensured low operating costs.

In baseball's early years, a financially successful operation relied on daily cash flow. Teams could not afford off-days, so leagues depended on an even number of franchises and short travel between cities. Still, even the larger cities could not always be counted on to support a team. Austin, in particular, developed a reputation to drop out of the league quickly if faced with financial difficulties. In order to ensure a geographically balanced six-club league, owners soon found themselves considering Texas's second-tier cities. The twin cities of Sherman and Denison, with growing populations and well-developed railroad systems, represented logical first choices, but league organizers didn't realize the depth of the rivalry between the Grayson County neighbors.

CHAPTER 4

SHERMAN, DENISON AND THE FENCELESS FRONTIER

People went to Sherman for religion; they went to Denison for fun.

Just a few miles and one narrow creek separated Grayson County's twin cities, but in terms of ambition, they couldn't have been more different. Sherman favored culture. Denison aggressively chased commerce. Sherman maintained order. Denison thrived on chaos. While the two cities could have complemented each other and become a force in North Texas to rival Dallas and Fort Worth, more often than not, they fostered a less than cooperative, if not contentious, relationship.

Culture, topography and politics all divided Grayson County. Nature split the county into two distinct regions: the prairie in the east and the cross timbers in the west. The cross timbers, a dense, wooded thicket and a natural barrier to development and transportation, attracted immigrants from the forested areas of the upper south who felt at home in settling on its eastern edge. On the other hand, the prairie's open range for farming and ranching appealed to those from the Midwest. Settlers followed the expected pattern, south divided from north even within the same county.

While topography divided Grayson County, the transportation routes it created helped bring the county together. Over the centuries, Native Americans had developed trails and paths crisscrossing the area, all in an effort to avoid the seemingly impenetrable cross timbers. When the settlers adopted these routes for transportation, Grayson County became one of the most easily traveled in Texas. Accessibility bred cooperation among settlers, but it also created paths to conflict.

Sherman, Texas, circa 1905. *Author's collection.*

Dr. John Brooke, one of Grayson County's earliest settlers, described the view from the front of his cabin as one of "prairies and groves of timber, surpassing, in my idea, the beauties of the sea." Brooke's county offered opportunity, a resource waiting for settlement and economic development. In 1846, commissioners of the new county placed development in motion, establishing a county seat in its geographic center. Eventually located near the "Big Spring" and its abundant water and timber resources, the commissioners named the community in honor of Texas Revolution hero and railroad pioneer Sidney Sherman.

For several years, Sherman consisted mostly of a "row of clapboard houses, a few saloons, and a double log house with a few trees." County leaders conducted business in the shade of a large pecan tree serving as the courthouse, bank, post office and church. By the early 1850s, Sherman's population reached four hundred, but both Preston and Kentuckytown in opposite ends of the county boasted more residents.

Sherman's slow growth continued through the early to mid-1850s. In 1857, when the city sported a few stores and a hotel, it garnered a stop on the Butterfield Line, a stagecoach company carrying mail from St. Louis to the West Coast. The Butterfield fueled Sherman's first economic boom, and property values soared. The stagecoach and cattle drives along the

Shawnee Trail made Sherman an important stop for those crossing the Red River in either direction. But even a growing county seat could not unify Grayson County.

Like all of North Texas, secession deeply divided Grayson County. Midwestern immigrants largely opposed leaving the Union, while those from the South, particularly the few who owned slaves, favored establishing a Confederate States of America. By 1860, as cotton and its labor-intensive harvest overtook corn and grain as North Texas's most important crop, Grayson County's slave population grew to 1,300. Slave owners remained in the minority, but political power rested with the cotton farmers, and a cotton harvest needed a strong slave presence.

While Grayson County and most of the northern tier of Texas counties voted against secession, Texas as a whole voted in favor by a margin of nearly four to one. Secessionists pressured those opposing slavery to remain quiet or leave the area, and many chose the latter. A group of pro-secession Texans terrorized some who stayed, eventually hanging forty men accused of organizing the "Loyal Union League" at Gainesville, about thirty miles west of Sherman. Grayson County organized Confederate regiments, and during the war, much of North Texas's male population traveled east to fight for the Rebel cause. Four years later, the survivors returned home, defeated but still enthusiastic about the opportunities Texas offered.

Texas didn't suffer the physical destruction of the southern states east of the Mississippi River, but it couldn't escape economic hardship. Property values plummeted across North Texas, and those who had not fought in the war suffered from frequent Indian raids. By 1870, though, Grayson County sat on the edge of changes that would fuel rapid growth and rivalries lasting well into the next century.

By the time the Houston and Texas Central Railroad reached Dallas in 1872, the Katy continued building steadily southward through Indian Territory. The two lines were destined to meet in Grayson County, but where and at what expense remained to be determined. The HTC, owning the preferred right of way through the county, clearly held the upper hand.

The HTC and the Katy represented the United States' westernmost rail lines. Their ultimate junction in North Texas would be a historical commercial development, with the site sure to be counted among the nation's most important cities. Communities having experienced the railroad boom, though, knew

This abandoned Texas and Pacific Railroad right of way shuttled early Texas Leaguers between Paris, Sherman and points beyond. *Karen Rutherford photo.*

the industry brought nuisances along with prosperity. Drunkards, gamblers, outlaws, ruffians and general ne'er-do-wells followed railroads in search of money, recreation and other "advantages." The inevitable HTC-Katy junction would likely have double its share of undesirables. Regardless, most city leaders fought hard to attract railroads, the advantages far outweighing any inconvenience. Unlike some cities, though, Sherman had high standards, and the Katy found its leaders difficult to persuade.

Initially, the Katy hoped to connect with the HTC at Red River City, a small outpost on the Texas side of the river where a ferry had operated since the 1850s. The Red River City connection required the two railroads to share the cost of a bridge, but with the HTC controlling the right of way, it stood on firm footing and refused to cooperate. The Katy was left to its own devices as it entered Grayson County. The best and cheapest route to Sherman already in its competitor's hands, the Katy laid its own route, one hampered by topography and construction obstacles. Katy executives feared the cost of building to Sherman might bankrupt the railroad. Again, Grayson County became a battleground as the two railroad empires fought for the industry's future in North Texas.

County historians dispute the reason the Katy did not ultimately establish itself in Sherman. While some claim Sherman's leaders refused to provide the financial incentive the Katy demanded, others noted that the city already had its hands full with the HTC and didn't need the added hassle of a second railroad. On the other hand, Sherman officials couldn't possibly support a second railroad terminal in the county that would diminish their city's status as the commercial center. At one point, Sherman officials even filed an injunction to prevent the "unchartered, illegal, and bankrupt" Katy from entering Texas. The legal effort failed, and the Katy continued its plans to cross the river.

Sherman leaders receive much blame for not securing the Katy, but some historians suspect the railroad's executives never really wanted a terminal in the city. A railroad terminal meant big business, and Katy executives knew it. Many believe the company wanted to build its own town and offset rail construction costs by selling lots to the businesses a railroad terminal naturally attracted. In the end, this is exactly what happened.

Using surrogates operating under the auspices of buying a cattle ranch, the secretive Denison Town Company quietly purchased thousands of acres a few miles north of Sherman. Word soon leaked that the company was actually an outgrowth of the Katy Railroad and planned to locate its major machine shop, maintenance yard and storage facility on the property, dividing the remaining acreage into commercial and residential lots. By late 1872, the community of Denison, three thousand residents strong, sat on land that only months earlier had been open range. Unfortunately for Denison but to the delight of Sherman, construction couldn't keep up with population growth. Denison's living conditions became deplorable.

Today's urban planners would never believe the dense area of tents, saloons, brothels and cockfighting pits filling Denison represented one of America's first community planning efforts. Main Street, a broad muddy thoroughfare, held the distinction as a business district only in name. The Denison Town Company reserved all authority to issue permits and tax saloons, bawdy houses, brothels, gambling halls and gaming houses and allowed only the most pristine to set up shop on Main Street. Few met the standard, and downtown Denison remained largely deserted. Denisonians conducted their real business on Skiddy, a ravine just a block south of Main Street.

Lined with crude shacks and tents and wreaking of hogs, cattle and the filth they left behind, Skiddy, or "Rat Alley," thrived on prostitution, whiskey, gambling and general rowdiness. Whites, blacks and Indians intermingled along Skiddy, and violence ran rampant. Just four miles from the lawless Indian Territory, outlaws made Denison a makeshift outpost, large enough to provide supplies and entertainment but close enough to the border to allow a quick escape.

Within a year, Denison had proven itself to be exactly as Shermanites predicted. Seemingly, all of Denison was involved in swindling, gambling, stealing or some other immoral activity. Sherman leaders gloated at Denison's growing pains, but some merchants couldn't pass up the opportunities the new city offered. The most enterprising placed their businesses atop logs and rolled them northward to serve the new residents. By 1875, Denison gained population, but its density bred disease, and a cholera outbreak killed many citizens and taxed the young community's resources.

Throughout the 1870s, railroads continued building toward Grayson County, and an underlying mutual benefit between Sherman and Denison took shape. The HTC and Katy eventually met at Denison, a connection finally tying Texas to the rest of the country. In fact, Denison became one of America's key junctions, a base for travel to all points north, south, east and west via rail. Within a decade, no fewer than seven railroads had established terminals in Denison, while others—including the Texas Pacific, Frisco, Santa Fe and Cotton Belt—converged on Sherman. Eventually, skilled railroad workers and their families outnumbered vagrants, and the rule of law took hold. Railroads fostered culture, education, business and industry, and both Sherman and Denison reaped their benefits. But progress did little to repair division, and a deep community rivalry continued.

Sherman and Denison stood against everything the other prized. Although Denison established the first free school in Texas, Sherman became the leader in culture and education. It built a reputation as the "Athens of Texas" by attracting numerous academies and colleges, most significantly Austin College, relocated from Huntsville in 1876. Sherman prided itself on its opera houses, theaters, prominent hotels and high moral standards. City leaders boasted that Sherman chose "culture over the Katy."

Denison mocked Sherman as the "Holy City," conservative and with a church on every street corner. Sherman may have prospered among the social set, but Denison believed itself to be the commercial center of Grayson County. Denison weathered the economic depression of the 1870s better than Sherman with its larger railroad facilities attracting cotton and cattle-based commerce. The city's local laws and regulations favored business development, and Denison temporarily replaced Sherman as the cotton exchange capital of Texas. Its leaders did little to downplay the city's reputation for saloons and gambling halls.

While Sherman and Denison eventually learned to reap the benefits of the other, the community rivalry ran deep, fueled by local newspapers. The *Sherman Daily Register* tossed a steady barrage of attacks northward, referring to Denison as "Little Denny" and its "Sad Little Neighbor." *Register* publishers editorialized Sherman should fight for itself and forget about the needs of nearby communities, openly predicting the eventual demise of Denison.

The *Denison Daily News* did not shy from the rivalry. Editors routinely flaunted Denison's prosperity and rapid growth, poking fun at Sherman's insistence on favoring morality over progressive development. Sherman shot back that the eventual construction of a passenger system connecting the two cities would allow Denisonians to cross the creek and see a "real town"—one that would soon render "poor, deluded" Denison an afterthought.

The newspaper battle aside, the deep divisions between Sherman, Denison and Grayson County in general fueled a fierce baseball competition. Denison's Blue Stockings squared off against the Sherman Resolutes many times annually, with newspaper accounts indicating Sherman's normally getting the best of its rival on the diamond. The Blue Stockings' failure on the ball field merely motivated the Gate City Baseball Association to construct the briefly heralded finest ballpark in Texas in Forest Park. If they couldn't beat the Resolutes on the diamond, the Blue Stockings would surely beat them at the gate.

It was not until 1888 that the *Denison Daily News* editor suggested the two cities bury the hatchet. If Sherman and Denison cooperated, he wrote, they could establish twin cities of fifty thousand citizens each, at that point enough to challenge Dallas and Fort Worth for supremacy in North Texas. The editorial reference to "the hatchet" became somewhat prophetic, as years later, Sherman and Denison high schools came to challenge each other in the annual "Battle of the Axe" on the gridiron. The game remains one of Texas's oldest football rivalries and has been labeled among the best high school sports rivalries in America. In a time when it has become difficult to recognize where Sherman ends and Denison begins, the Battle of the Axe keeps the original community animosities alive at least once a year.

By 1890, Denison surpassed Sherman in population, outnumbering its neighbor by fewer than one thousand residents. Denison boasted a cigar factory, two breweries, three newspapers, sixteen doctors and eighteen saloons. With an overland railroad payroll of over $1 million, a streetcar company also operated within the city. Sherman, on the other hand, had little trouble keeping pace with its neighbor. The Sherman Oil and Cotton Company operated the largest cottonseed oil plant in the world, and later in the decade, the Birge-Forbes Cotton Company became the largest cotton brokerage in the South. The city also offered its own streetcar system to shuttle citizens to theaters attracting the likes of musician John Phillip Sousa and lecturer and presidential candidate William Jennings Bryan. While the two cities seemed very different on a local level, to the rest of Texas, they may as well have been one in the same. Sherman and Denison were soon forever linked in the public psyche as North Texas's twin cities, and despite efforts to distinguish themselves, the two became enjoined in an on-and-off relationship that helped build the Texas League.

CHAPTER 5

1895: THE TEXAS LEAGUE'S FIRST FORAY INTO A SECOND-TIER CITY

With its college, high school and amateur ball clubs popular diversions, Sherman officials set sights on professional baseball soon after the Texas League formed. They first attempted to gain a franchise in 1892, but John McCloskey insisted the Texas baseball circuit consist of only the state's largest cities. McCloskey believed small communities could not support professional baseball and would drain league resources. In Sherman's defense, if the first few seasons of the Texas League had proven anything, it was that no city was immune to failure. In fact, several club owners had proven they would bail at adversity's first sign. A successful league depended on stable leadership, and as the league sought to reorganize, officials believed they had found a proven leader when one of the best-known baseball men in the country arrived in Texas.

Ted Sullivan may have been born an Irishman, but he promoted America's game better than any man alive. Born in Dublin in 1851, Sullivan immigrated to the United States around the time of the Civil War, settling near Milwaukee. By 1870, he pitched and captained the St. Mary's Academy and College club in Kansas. Sullivan, though, set his sights on the big picture and didn't confine his baseball interests to his alma mater. Each summer, he returned to Wisconsin to manage a local semipro team and promote baseball's growth at every opportunity.

While Ted Sullivan may not have been the finest ballplayer of his day, he had a keen eye for talent. In 1874, a young student from Chicago arrived at St. Mary's, shipped to the school by his concerned father who believed baseball

Above: Baseball pioneer Ted Sullivan. *Author's collection.*

Opposite: Major League Hall of Famer Charles Comiskey, a talent discovered by Ted Sullivan. *Author's collection.*

had become more important than his studies. Sullivan immediately recognized the youngster's ability and recruited him for the team. To his father's surprise (or maybe chagrin), the young pitcher Charles Comiskey went on to a long baseball career, eventually owning the Chicago White Sox and becoming one of the sport's most iconic figures.

Comiskey represented Ted Sullivan's first foray into the business of scouting, a method of locating, signing and developing baseball talent Sullivan himself pioneered. He continued to perfect his system throughout the 1870s as he organized independent clubs in Iowa. In 1879, Sullivan became fully invested in baseball, founding the Northwest League. A staunch supporter of salary caps, Sullivan insisted in treating the Northwest League as a true minor league, with no intention of competing for players with major-league franchises. Sullivan's frugality made him a legend in minor-league circles, and his approach toward signing undeveloped talent became the basis for the tiered system in place today.

Throughout the 1880s, Sullivan cultivated his name and his sport. Baseball owners took note of his knack for spotting talent, and during the decade, he managed three major-league teams to a 132-132 career record. Despite his mediocrity in the big leagues, Sullivan flourished in the minors. He invested in fledgling leagues across the country, staying aboard long enough to put a league on firm footing before moving on. By the early 1890s, Sullivan settled in the Tennessee and Georgia area, joining the Southern League, one of minor-league baseball's most legendary circuits. Southerners' interest in baseball impressed Sullivan, and he became convinced the sport could succeed in the still-untapped Texas market. Texas's geography, large cities and extensive railroad system offered all the attributes a baseball league needed. By late 1894, Sullivan had traveled to Fort Worth to meet with local baseball enthusiasts, having every intention of leaving the city with the framework for a new Texas League in place.

While previous attempts to establish professional baseball in Texas had failed, Ted Sullivan remained undeterred. Early Texas League officials knew how to play baseball, but they had no experience promoting the sport as a business. Sullivan had a keen business sense, knew the importance of salary caps and personally supervised every penny spent. While major-league players traveled in luxurious Pullman cars, Sullivan's teams traveled coach. Eventually, "Sullivan's Pullmans," as they were known, became the standard method of minor-league travel. Sullivan fully appreciated previous Texas owners' preoccupation with the "jump" and knew success required a geographically compact league. Likewise, his frequent travels educated him in the railroad business, and Sullivan learned to negotiate special fares for both players and spectators. He brought all of this knowledge to Texas and insisted it be incorporated in the league he proposed to field in 1895.

As the 1894 season took shape, the Texas League's original cities remained the most populated and viable baseball towns. Still, smaller cities like Sherman and Denison lobbied for admittance. Realizing the slim chances of the two cities of six thousand residents being accepted separately, Sherman and Denison submitted an application for a joint franchise. Lewis M. Legg, a fireman with the Katy Railroad, championed the effort as the tandem competed for league slots against the likes of Shreveport and New Orleans. Other owners supported Legg's argument that Sherman-Denison, along with Dallas, Fort Worth and Waco, would balance the south Texas teams of Houston, Galveston, Austin and San Antonio. Likewise, South Texas owners, led by George Dermoddy of Galveston, vehemently opposed franchises in Louisiana, giving Sherman-Denison an inside track to obtain a franchise.

As planning for 1895 continued, the cities in contention for two of the eight franchises traded barbs. Northern clubs didn't see Shreveport as a great distance to travel; in fact, the city was a shorter jump from Dallas than some of those in South Texas. Likewise, once a team arrived in Shreveport, New Orleans was only a short train ride away. The Crescent City, though, carried baggage into the competition. Under National Agreement rules, a sanctioned franchise held a no-compete claim within a fifty-mile radius of its home city. With a New Orleans franchise already in the Southern League, any entry into the Texas League would have to first obtain that team's permission, a virtual impossibility considering the economic times. By January, New Orleans dropped its bid, leaving just nine cities in the running.

League president J.C. McNealus faced an unnerving decision in selecting a city able to maintain a competitive circuit.

With an even number of teams required for scheduling purposes, one worthy city would be left out of the 1895 Texas League circuit. Waco franchise promoters soon proved unable to overcome its city's ban on Sunday baseball, and its association dropped its effort to acquire a team, essentially leaving Sherman-Denison as the final franchise. Corsicana officials offered a late pitch for a team, but like Waco, they faced local opposition to Sunday baseball. Ultimately the well-organized Sherman Baseball Association prevailed. In fact, the association eventually drove Denison away, and Sherman claimed the franchise as its own. With a professional team secure, Sherman established itself as one of the state's most active baseball towns, the Texas League franchise joining two high school teams, a number of amateur clubs, an African American team and the Austin College club.

The Sherman Baseball Association leaders included future Texas League president C.P. Gregory, north Texas Jewish leader Max Eppstein and Hugh Perry, a local merchant who would eventually establish the infamous Texas School Book Depository in Dallas. Streetcar company owner and Civil War veteran Will Batsell played a prominent role in acquiring the franchise, offering his property as a ball field. Batsell's grandson Charles Batsell Winstead, eventually the FBI agent credited with killing John Dillinger, spoke eloquently of his grandfather's park in his letter to the *Sherman Daily Register*:

> *My grandpa has a park; it is called "Batsell's park," and he has about twenty deer in it, besides seven little ones with spots on them. And, grandpa has a pair of peafowls. They have two little ones that look just like little turkeys. One of them hopped into the slop. It did it two times, and grandpa had to get it out.—Charlie Batsell Winstead, 5 years old, 1896*

Will Batsell's streetcar business stood to profit from shuttling spectators to the park on southern outskirts of town, and with his teenage son becoming active in the sport, Batsell had plenty of incentive to support the local association. The association warmly received Batsell's offer of a ballpark and also rewarded the efforts of Lewis Legg, naming him manager of the Texas League's first small-city franchise, the Sherman Orphans.

Manager Legg quickly went to work assembling a team and wasted no time boasting of his success, noting, "Prospects are very bright for base ball in Sherman. We have things in first-class shape. I have a number of men signed and expect to have a winning team from the start."

Sherman inaugurated professional baseball on April 5, 1895, in the middle of a weeklong dust storm, losing two of three games to a team from Alexandria, Louisiana. The real treat for Grayson County fans, though, took place on April 14, when the Katys, a railroad-sponsored semipro team from Denison, came to town. Still fuming at Sherman's late move to drop Denison from its Texas League plans, many Denisonians made the trek to Sherman for the game. Over one thousand spectators turned out in the ongoing dust storm to watch the local team dominate the Katys 18–3. Regardless of the fact that Sherman fielded professional ballplayers against railroad workers who spent most days laboring in a hot rail yard, the outcome thrilled local fans. The *Dallas Morning News* described the Sherman club as in excellent shape, well disciplined under the leadership of Lewis Legg.

Sherman's entry into the Texas League came in the earliest stages of the Deadball Era, a period of professional baseball unofficially beginning at the start of the twentieth century. Low-powered offenses and few home runs marked the Deadball Era, with the game dominated by managerial strategy and speed on the base paths. Home run leaders of the era often hit fewer than ten per season, most of them of the inside-the-park variety. Teams found success on the base paths, and a roster with a few speedy base runners often spelled the difference between elite and run-of-the-mill teams.

Deadball Era pitchers relied on trickery and the comfort of knowing power hitters were few and far between. Over the years, as the pitcher's on-field position evolved from a simple box to a plate to a mound, pitchers searched for any advantage they could find. Doctoring the baseball was an accepted part of the game, and pitchers often scuffed and cut a ball to the point that it danced on its way to the hitter. One ball lasted an entire game unless lost, with spectators returning the ball to the field if batted into the stands. The loosely wound balls of the day took a beating and softened considerably as the games went along, and by the latter innings, even the most powerful hitters had difficulty driving the ball into the outfield.

Minor-league ballplayers of the Deadball Era might have exhibited speed on the base paths, but they had an unsurpassed capacity for committing errors when in the field. Poorly maintained diamonds marked by rough infields and usually void of grass made all fielding plays anything but routine. Team errors often exceeded a half dozen a game, with as many as a dozen common. Games played in cities like Sherman, where a well-groomed ballpark had yet to be established, frequently sported the highest number of errors. The fielding miscues only benefited pitchers' statistics, whose ERAs remained low as errors led to many unearned runs.

The 1895 Sherman Orphans. *Courtesy Grayson County GenWeb.*

Lewis Legg organized his franchise around a core of ballplayers including first baseman Charles Douglass, shortstop Billy Oswald, outfielders Frank Keys and William "Kid" Nance, catcher William B. Douglass and pitchers James Maloney, Virgil Lee Garvin and George Gilpatrick. Adding to what Manager Legg thought a potent lineup, the day before the season began, the Orphans signed original Texas Leaguer "Big" Mike O'Connor as outfielder and team captain. The future Texas League Hall of Famer carried statewide respect as a powerful hitter and strategist and immediately made the Sherman squad a force in the league.

The exhibition games behind them, the Orphans opened the Texas League season at home on April 20 against Fort Worth. The Sherman Baseball Association organized a gala celebration, including a parade featuring both teams, city officials, clergy, Austin College faculty and a band. The parade route stretched from the city plaza all the way to Batsell's Park, where spectators packed the new grandstand, many having traveled to the ballpark in Will Batsell's mule-powered streetcars. Navosta's Virgil Lee Garvin threw the season's first pitch, and the crowd cheered wildly when the first inning ended with the home team in front 4–1. As the afternoon wore on, though,

Fort Worth took advantage of seven Sherman errors and finished with a 9–4 victory. The following day, the Orphans led again, carrying a one-run lead into the bottom of the ninth inning before falling 6–4. Sherman fans proved fickle, and only a few turned out the following day to see the Orphans claim their first win behind Lee Garvin's ten strikeouts.

Following the opening series, Dallas visited Sherman, sweeping three games. Dallas owner Ted Sullivan, obviously concerned about holding his new league together, tried to boost the locals' spirits, stating there wasn't a stronger team in the league, and before the season ended, the Orphans were sure to make the league favorites sweat. Both the Orphans and their rooters quickly forgot Sullivan's kind words when Sherman closed the month with three consecutive losses by scores of 21–20, 14–3 and 24–20.

Errors plagued Sherman during the season's first six weeks. Sherman fielders often committed six or eight errors in a single game, but the most disappointing performance occurred on May 2 with Lee Garvin on the mound in Dallas. Garvin pitched masterfully, allowing just three hits and being labeled a "diaphanous twirler" with "crooked and fiery curves" by the *Dallas Morning News*. Despite his efforts, the teams entered the ninth inning tied at three, Sherman's three errors having kept Dallas in the game. With Garvin still pitching strongly in the ninth, Sherman appeared unbeatable if it could only score a run, but the Orphans' infield fell apart before getting another crack at bat. Four Sherman errors and three Dallas runs later, Sherman left the field with a 6–3 loss and a frustrated pitcher in Lee Garvin.

Virgil Lee Garvin, "the Navosta Tarantula," a terror both on and off the field. *Author's collection.*

The Orphans' play disgusted the Sherman Baseball Association. Although their team led the league in attendance, association leaders knew Sherman baseball fans would not continue buying tickets to see a losing team. Plus, baseball men in Denison pressured the league to allow them to join Sherman in a joint venture, something the Sherman Association viewed as a last resort. Desperate for a change of fortunes, the association took action, firing manager Lewis Legg and promoting Mike O'Connor to the position.

O'Connor saw little success in his first week as manager as the Orphans continued to struggle, posting a 2-5 record on a road trip to Shreveport and Galveston. On May 13, though, O'Connor's managerial skills took hold. Sherman traveled to Houston, San Antonio, Dallas and Austin, taking eight of nine games. They then returned home and rolled off twelve consecutive wins, the pitching staff holding opponents to two or fewer runs in seven of the contests. In the middle of the streak, the Orphans and the Sherman Baseball Association received a boost when league president McNealus resigned over a dispute involving treatment of umpires, declaring he would never again attend a professional baseball game. In his place, team owners appointed C.P. Gregory, vice-president of the Sherman Baseball Association, an apparent vote of confidence in the association's efforts.

Whatever support Gregory may have offered from the president's desk couldn't save the Orphans from a June swoon. The winning stretch burst against Dallas, with the Giants posting 25–8 and 14–2 victories in Sherman. The losses sucked the wind from the Orphans' sails, and the team won just two of its next fifteen games, ending June with an eleven-game losing streak, its 28-31 record good for only fifth place in the eight-team league.

With league standings lopsided and fearing losing the interest of fans in Sherman and other "tail-end" cities, Texas League owners elected to start anew in July with a second-half season. The first-half winner, Ted Sullivan's Dallas Giants, would challenge the second-half winner in a championship series to be held at season's end. The first and second half arrangement became popular with Texas League fans, and it remains in use today, giving even a struggling team a chance to reverse its fortunes at mid-season.

While the less successful teams struggled to attract fans and pay salaries, league officials recognized a familiar crisis brewing. Several players damaged the league's reputation by frequenting saloons, and team owners feared their exploits would turn off the fan base, particularly the ladies, a group the league had begun actively courting. The owners quickly convened, publicly denouncing immoral activity among ballplayers and threatening any player not abiding to the standards with blacklisting. The 1895 Texas League, they said, would not fall victim to the same player issues that had led to the demise of the earlier leagues.

While the league mentioned no players by name, Sherman pitching ace Lee Garvin was undoubtedly among the top offenders, fostering a reputation to follow him throughout his career. Garvin, who eventually played seven major-league seasons, became widely known as one of professional baseball's most notorious drinkers and troublemakers. Over the course of his career, witnesses accused Garvin of beating a team secretary and traveling salesman in New Jersey, shooting a Milwaukee shoeshine man for unsatisfactory service, stabbing a Chicago man in a saloon fight and shooting both a friend and police officer during an argument. Despite his uncontrolled temper and penchant for violence, Garvin never faced criminal charges. In fact, Milwaukee police accepted his defense of "Texans don't like niggers" and refused to press charges in the shooting of the shoeshine man. Dubbed the "Texas Demon" and "Navosta Tarantula," Garvin took his street tenacity to the pitcher's box, posting a career ERA of 2.72. Unfortunately, he pitched for teams with notoriously poor offenses and finished with a big-league record of 58-96, thirteen of his victories shutouts. Baseball historian Bill James listed Garvin as the "hard-luck" pitcher of the early 1900s and possibly of all time. Had he received offensive support, James noted, Garvin had the potential to be a superstar.

In Sherman, Garvin shared pitching duties with George Kilpatrick and James "Curley" Maloney. The trio offered mixed results. When the offense came to life, the Orphans might generate enough runs to pull out a win, but on other occasions, the pitchers never gave their teammates a chance. In the season's first half, the pitching staff gave up ten or more runs nine times, including the lopsided losses that ultimately led to Lewis Legg's firing. The offense, on the other hand, scored three runs or fewer thirteen times, all in losses. The infield offered little support, posting fielding errors at a seemingly record pace.

The Orphans started the second half of the 1895 season with a new manager in Harry Gatewood. Before binding contracts, players and managers alike shifted teams on a whim, sometimes even between games of a double-header. Mike O'Connor left his job in Sherman to play for a potential champion in Dallas, providing an opening for Gatewood, manager of the Western League's St. Joseph franchise, to resign his position and move to Sherman. Gatewood led the team to an 18-17 record, highlighted by Lee Garvin's thirteen-inning, 2–1 victory over Shreveport on July 3.

Unfortunately for Harry Gatewood, by mid-July, Lee Garvin left the lineup with an apparent injury and pitched only sporadically the rest of the season. With his star pitcher out of the lineup, Gatewood soon followed O'Connor out of Sherman, replaced by catcher Bill "Klondike" Douglass. The Orphans welcomed Douglass's promotion with consecutive wins over Austin, scoring forty-five runs in the two games. Events in South Texas, however, soon began to overshadow any signs of life Sherman might offer. By early August, the South Texas teams became insolvent, and the Texas League began to disintegrate. San Antonio, Houston and Austin all folded in a single week, forcing the league to drop Shreveport to maintain a balanced schedule. Decimated by injuries, the Orphans offense all but disappeared, and the team lost nine of ten games, finishing the second half of the season with a disappointing 26-32 record.

Despite the Orphans won-loss record, the Sherman Baseball Association considered the 1895 season an overall success. Although finishing fourth and last among the teams finishing the season, Mike O'Connor's .350 and Charlie Douglass's .339 batting averages tantalized local fans along with Kid Nance's forty-three extra-base hits and Klondike Douglass's thirty-seven stolen bases. On the mound, George Gilpatrick won eighteen games, outpacing James Maloney's fifteen wins. Hard-luck Garvin, though pitching valiantly, finished with a won-loss record of just 12-19 despite a low ERA. The Sherman Baseball Association, though, did not measure success only on the field.

Despite stretches of poor play, four managers and twelve cancelled or postponed games, Sherman residents turned out to support their team. On several occasions, the *Dallas Morning News* reported attendance in excess of one thousand, and the most loyal fans took advantage of special railroad excursions and followed the team on road trips to Dallas and Fort Worth. Local businessmen like Will Batsell and Hugh Perry reaped the benefits of the public enthusiasm, with Batsell's streetcar company ringing in profits and Perry unable to keep his store stocked with baseball equipment. The sport became so popular in the heavily religious city of Sherman that a number of youngsters broke into Perry's store long enough to steal a ball, a bat and a few mitts. It seemed that when it came to baseball, nothing was sacred.

Most importantly for the Texas League, Sherman's success proved that small towns could thrive on the circuit, and its showing offered owners confidence to move forward with a league composed of the state's six largest cities and two second-tier towns. Even before the 1895 season ended, those smaller cities jockeyed for position, led by Sherman's longtime rival to the north.

CHAPTER 6

1896: A RIVALRY CUT SHORT

John L. Ward was a professional baseball man only by association. William H. Ward, John's brother, owned the Texas League's Fort Worth franchise and had been involved in amateur and professional baseball since leaving Grayson County in the mid-1880s. John, on the other hand, had little interest in his brother's baseball business endeavors, choosing instead to enjoy the sport as an amateur player and manager. He bounced from job to job, working as a railroad engineer in Denison and a cigar salesman in Fort Worth. By 1890, John, like Will Batsell and others before him, recognized the profit possibilities in commercial recreation, but Ward didn't look to baseball. Instead, he saw a future in the seedier side of recreation and purchased Fort Worth's White Elephant Saloon. Over the next few years, Ward built the White Elephant into one of the Southwest's premier bars and billiards/gambling halls. Despite its success, John found the business unsatisfying and soon became restless. Leaving the saloon in his brother's hands, John moved to Idaho and worked odd jobs for a few years. In 1896, he returned to Fort Worth and, for lack of better prospects, assisted William with his baseball team, fully unaware of the role the sport would soon play in his life.

The dust had barely settled on the 1895 season before Will Batsell and C.P. Gregory traveled to Fort Worth for the first meeting to organize the 1896 Texas League. The Sherman Baseball Association knew the previous season's success offered no guarantee of a new franchise. Though not yet a serious contender for admittance, in 1895, Denison's leaders flirted with failing franchises in San Antonio, Shreveport and Houston, and Batsell

Although Will Batsell never saw long-term success of a Texas League franchise in Sherman, he did live to see the league build itself as a source of Major League talent. *Karen Rutherford photo.*

and Gregory arrived in Fort Worth to protect Sherman's interests. The Denison Streetcar Company, undoubtedly encouraged by Batsell's success in Sherman, announced plans to erect a grandstand and extend the rail line to a new ballpark. From all appearances, Sherman and Denison would renew their rivalry, this time for the rights to an 1896 Texas League franchise.

Aside from Denison promoters, the Sherman Baseball Association also battled Texas League officials. The influential William H. Ward supported Denison's effort to obtain a team, noting that even though the population of Sherman and Denison combined was less than half of Dallas, the many small towns in surrounding Grayson County would take advantage of the area's extensive transportation network and support teams in both cities. Ward suggested Sherman and Denison be admitted to the league as separate franchises, with a schedule organized so neither would play home games on the same date. He also pointed out the great local interest to be generated when the teams faced each other. All of Grayson County would turn out, he assured. Batsell and Gregory were far from convinced such an arrangement would work, but Gregory no longer carried the influence of the league president's desk, placing Sherman at a disadvantage in negotiations.

If the 1896 Texas League was to be successful, it would be without Ted Sullivan's baseball expertise. Sullivan once again got the itch to move about and left Texas behind for New England. With C.P. Gregory having been only a temporary president, the remaining owners coveted league secretary James Nolan for the position, but he not only expressed disinterest but also spoke of his disgust with Texas baseball. The Texas League, he said, was too disorganized to control and the president's position not worth the pay or trouble involved. With no obvious successor to Gregory, on October 1, William H. Ward nominated his brother as temporary league president. The owners unanimously elected John L. Ward to the position in spite of his lack of interest or experience. With "temporary" soon removed from his title, Ward began to organize the 1896 franchises.

Unlike previous seasons, the 1896 Texas League drew attention from many potential cities. In addition to the six stalwarts, at least eight cities expressed interest in fielding teams. Sherman, Denison, Waco, Greenville, Corsicana, Terrell, Tyler and Paris entered a battle for two available franchises. League owners considered Sherman a virtual lock, and President Ward favored Paris as the eighth team. Waco and Corsicana, led by local businessman J. Doak Roberts, proposed a joint team with plans to split home games between the two cities. Though sportswriters considered both good baseball towns, neither allowed Sunday baseball, and owners never gave Roberts's proposal serious consideration. Among the remaining cities, Denison drew the most support, undoubtedly due to the savings of a short jump through North Texas. A Denison franchise meant the entire northern circuit would lie within a seventy-five-mile radius.

Once they assured Sherman a team, Texas League owners must have been encouraged at the vicious fight for the league's remaining franchise. Terrell and Greenville, both led by railroad mogul Edward Howland Robinson (E.H.R.) Green, promoted themselves on railroad backing and the railroad-baseball success story. The Denison Street Car Company countered with $500, a ballpark, a $2,000 stock investment and the guarantee of Sunday baseball. Likewise, Paris offered a stock company and a ballpark near the railroad. Former league president McNealus, apparently once again watching professional baseball and a Denison supporter, insisted Paris wanted games to be fixed in its favor if it was to guarantee gate receipts. So, the fight for the final franchise stretched into early 1896.

The Sherman Baseball Association covered its bases with a collaboration of civic leaders. With Will Batsell's ballpark and transportation system, banker C.B. Dorchester's financial backing, C.P. Gregory's executive experience and the support of the local power company, the association considered itself well positioned for another successful season. While Sherman spread its expertise among several individuals, Denison Baseball Association leader Leonidas Maughs rested his hopes on one man.

George Blackford, a banker by trade, moved to Texas from West Virginia in 1883. Active in a number of Denison enterprises—including the road and streetcar system, the Denison Building and Land Company, the Denison Compress and the ice company—locals respected Blackford as a citizen, businessman and civic leader. As a banker, he had contacts with many business owners who held an interest in a professional baseball team for the city, including the local power company. Even more importantly, though, Blackford had experience in commercial recreation as president of the Denison Driving Park and Fair Association. While Maughs offered a war hero's reputation and the prestige of both postmaster and a local attorney, George Blackford backed him with firsthand knowledge and influence in everything needed to attract a baseball franchise. Unlike the previous year, in 1896, Denison would not be denied.

While President Ward and former president McNealus negotiated with Denison for the league's eighth franchise, the railroad industry prepared for its role in the 1896 season. The Katy, Texas-Pacific, Santa Fe and Texas Central all announced special weekend excursion rates between small towns along the rail lines and Texas League cities. Even without a local team, the railroad arrangements ensured residents of Corsicana, Terrell and Greenville access to professional baseball games in North Texas for a reasonable rail fare and a game ticket. With the special fares, the railroad-baseball relationship grew even more mutually beneficial.

By the end of February, Maughs and Blackford secured enough money to support a Denison franchise and prepared to construct a ballpark. The streetcar company funded a two-thousand-seat grandstand at Fairbanks and Morton Streets and agreed to extend service directly to the park. By mid-March, the Denison Indians assembled and modeled their nifty maroon uniforms. Sherman, not to be outdone, announced a new team name, the Students, in honor of its reputation as a college town. They unveiled uniforms every bit as fancy as Denison's, with gray shirts adorned with maroon letters, navy blue pants and black caps with maroon stripes.

Denison started the season led by manager Cary Peacock, outfielder William Kohlne, shortstop Fred Valdois and second baseman Russ Steinhoff, but the Indians roster changed frequently as the season wore on. Mike O'Connor returned to Grayson County for a second consecutive

The 1896 Denison Indians. *Courtesy Grayson County GenWeb.*

season, this time signing with Denison. Pitcher James McGinnis anchored the Indians early, but Frank Quigg became Denison's winningest hurler. Quigg, a renowned troublemaker, fit perfectly with Denison's reputation as an untamed town. Later in his career, officials arrested Quigg for bribing opposing players and gambling offenses, but he cemented his reputation on New Year's Eve 1909. After obtaining his law license and retiring from baseball, Quigg joined a gang planning to rob a bank in Harrah, Oklahoma. Tipped off by informants, local marshals foiled the heist, shooting Frank Quigg and another member of the gang dead the moment they dismounted their horses. Thirteen years before the Harrah incident, though, Quigg pitched twelve of Denison's forty-one victories as stalwart of the Indians pitching staff. While Denison boasted mightily of its entry into the Texas League, Sherman initially took the competition in stride. With longtime professional catcher A.C. Jantzen, speedy infielder Paddy Lynch, future renowned artist William Van Dresser and returning third baseman Billy Oswald, the Students had a seemingly strong core lineup led by business manager Frank Ryan and field manager Harry Sage. Lee Garvin and

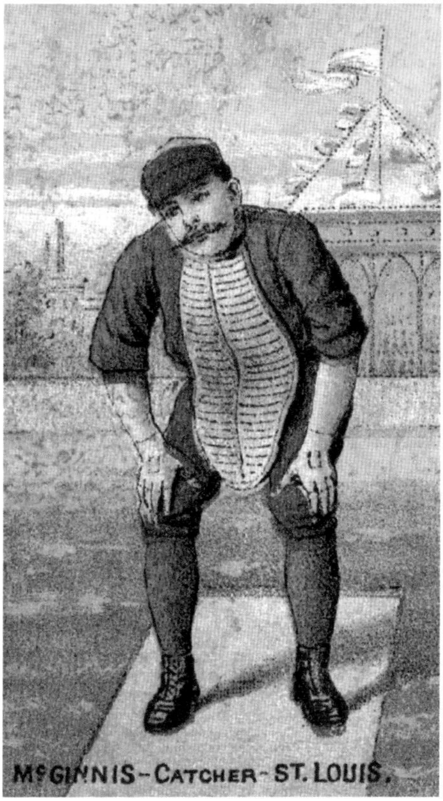

Left: Harry Sage, 1896 Denison field manager. *Author's collection.*

Right: James McGinnis, 1896 Denison pitcher/catcher. *Author's collection.*

George Gilpatrick returned to pitch for a second season, and after storming through a pre-season schedule against both professional and amateur teams, prospects for Sherman appeared bright.

When the season began on April 18, both Sherman and Denison sputtered out of the gate. The Students followed an opening day win in Fort Worth with five consecutive losses, while Denison lost its first six in uncompetitive fashion. On April 24, the two teams met in Denison for the first of many highly anticipated Grayson County showdowns.

The first game between the clubs left both Denison and Sherman fans anxious for more. With Denison holding a 10–7 lead in the eight inning, Sherman's A.C. Jantzen blasted a rare grand slam home run, propelling the Students to an 11–10 victory. The Students followed up with two more wins

A.C. Jantzen played for several minor-league teams in various leagues over the course of a long career. *Courtesy* Dallas Morning News.

over Denison, leaving the Indians with a 0-9 record and a new field manager in Mike O'Connor. By the time the two teams met again, Denison nursed a 3-12 record while Sherman rode a nine-game winning streak. The second series results matched the first, as Sherman claimed a three-game sweep. Both cities' newspapers undoubtedly drove hostilities to a higher level.

May 15, 1896, dawned gloomy in Grayson County. With the Sherman Students set to host the San Antonio Bronchos at Batsell's Park, a few miles up the rail line the Denison Indians prepared to face the Galveston Sand Crabs. Dallas weather observers had recorded a falling barometer for nearly forty-eight hours, and the forecast called for much-needed rain in North Texas. A strong cold front stretched just west of the area with temperatures behind the front nearly thirty degrees lower than those to the east. Grayson County lay on the front's warm side, and the strong southwest wind signaled the potential for heavy thunderstorms and the chance of crop-destructive hail.

All four teams in Grayson County suspected there would be no baseball that Friday afternoon. The wind howled throughout the day, and by late afternoon, the skies had darkened. Shortly after five o'clock, a reporter standing on the town square observed the swirling clouds southwest of Sherman forming into a funnel wrapped in heavy rainfall. Moments later, the reporter recalled, trees, branches and all sorts of debris flew through the air as a tornado tore through the city's western side. By six o'clock, the storm had passed, fortunately weakening before reaching Denison.

Sherman and Denison may have been rivals both on and off the field, but when it came to disasters like the tornado of 1896, Grayson County citizens became brothers. Denison doctors, construction workers, railroad men and those simply seeking to lend a hand quickly headed to Sherman to assist the injured, retrieve the dead and assess the damage. They found widespread devastation. The storm destroyed the entire west side of Sherman, with houses shattered or knocked from their foundations, businesses wiped out, roads blocked and bridges rendered impassable. The African American portion of town especially felt the storm's impact, and humanity won out over any sense of racism as all able bodies raced in to help.

All of Texas shared in Sherman's grief at the most deadly natural disaster since statehood. Other Texas League owners donated gate receipts to the relief effort; amateur ball clubs hosted benefit games across the state; and men, ladies and children sponsored fundraisers of all kinds. Donations poured in from as far away as Germany as news of the horrific storm spread across the globe. All told, the tornado killed seventy-three people, injured over two hundred more, destroyed fifty homes and a number of businesses and damaged countless other structures. Sherman's city leaders greatly appreciated the outpouring of support and knew the financial assistance saved the city from economic ruin.

From the standpoint of baseball, the tornado had limited initial impact. The storm toppled Sherman business manager Frank Ryan's house from its foundation, but his wife and children escaped uninjured. Sherman cancelled its series with San Antonio, though Denison went on to play its Saturday and Sunday games against Galveston. Neither of the ballparks suffered damage, and all appeared set for baseball to continue.

Despite logistics to play baseball still in place, the Sherman community had little interest or time for sport. Local residents had to bury the dead, repair or replace houses and reopen businesses. Few noticed when the Students left for a two-week road trip to South Texas, and even fewer paid attention to the sports pages reporting its seven losses in twelve games. By the time the Students returned to Grayson County for a series with Denison on May 31, enthusiasm for the rivalry had evaporated. Denison swept the series in convincing fashion, including a 27–9 pasting in the third game. The teams immediately traveled to Sherman for another series, the Students prevailing in two of the three games. By June 10, Sherman sported a .500 record after fifty games, and Denison had recovered from its atrocious start, now holding a 21-28 record.

After the game on June 9, Sherman players left the ballpark and headed to help with tornado recovery, find dinner or return to their boardinghouses. The Sherman Baseball Association, on the other hand, gathered for a meeting to discuss the events of the season. Since the tornado, attendance at Batsell's Park had dwindled, gate receipts no longer able to cover the visiting team's fifty-dollar guarantee. Likewise, the southern road trip's expenses exceeded the Students share of gate receipts, and the association found itself headed for insolvency. With tornado recovery expected to continue throughout the summer, baseball leaders recognized the meager prospects of fielding a financially successful baseball operation. On the evening of June 9, the association voted to disband the Sherman Students and wired their decision to Texas League president John Ward in Fort Worth.

President Ward claimed the decision caught him by surprise. He lamented the fact that Sherman officials failed to provide notice of the team's disbandment, leaving the future of its players—and that of the entire Texas League—in doubt. Had notice been provided, the league could have taken control of the team and kept it intact until a city willing to host the club could be found. Instead, the outright disbandment of the franchise freed Sherman's players from their contracts. On the morning of June 10, representatives of baseball clubs from across the South descended on Sherman to sign former Students to contracts.

President Ward did not take Sherman's withdrawal lightly. "To say that I am surprised hardly states the case," the heavyset, mustached leader told the *Dallas Morning News*. "Had Sherman given me any previous notice of its intention, I would have arranged a transfer to Paris or some other point, and not a game would have been missed."

While Ward claimed shock at Sherman's actions, Denison delighted in its neighbor's misfortune, its sympathy from the tornado apparently evaporated. The Denison newspaper bragged of its superiority on the diamond, noting that despite Sherman's insistence that Denison would not survive the season, it was Sherman that bailed out first.

While John L. Ward may have been outwardly shocked at Sherman's withdrawal, within twenty-four hours, he managed to arrange the franchise's move to Paris. Clearly, he knew the Students were not long for the league. As Ward originally supported a franchise in Paris when the 1896 league organized, it's likely he suspected neither Sherman nor Denison could support a team and had already made provisional arrangements for a Paris franchise should either falter. Regardless, as soon as Sherman disbanded, Ward announced the growing Lamar County seat as the franchise's new home. He wasted no time in commenting on the move, stating simply, "I will have nothing further to say other than that I have wired Paris and expect a reply every moment." Retiring to his office, he puffed on a cigar and stared through his window into the evening sky. The telegraph lines hummed along the Texas and Pacific Railroad right of way.

President Ward had set his eyes on Paris long before Sherman withdrew from the league. Geographically centered between Dallas and Texarkana, Paris's steady growth and increasing prominence as a railroad community offered Ward's league a chance to expand to another second-tier city. It also provided a future link to Texarkana, the gateway for expansion into Arkansas and Louisiana. Upon learning of Sherman's withdrawal, Ward offered the franchise to Paris physician Robert R. Walker, a former semipro ballplayer and strong influence in local affairs. Walker wasted no time and within hours arranged a local stock company funded primarily with railroad and traction company interests. The *Dallas Morning News*, just two days after announcing the departure of Sherman from the Texas League, heralded Paris's entry into the Texas League.

Sherman's decision to disband came while Paris baseball enthusiasts marveled at the play of Paris's semiprofessional team guided by Russ Steinhoff, the same ballplayer who had begun the season in Denison. Steinhoff, a light-hitting infielder, brought little in the way of baseball talent to Paris, but he knew the game and had a knack for organizing otherwise mediocre players into a formidable team. He also knew the arrival of professional baseball would end his semiprofessional team's ability to draw spectators, and he worked with Robert Walker to arrange for the Texas League to absorb most of Steinhoff's roster. Though without a quality third baseman, the semipro team essentially transferred en masse, joined by only a few of the Sherman players overlooked during the contract-frenzy descending on that city a day

Paris, Texas street scene, circa 1900. *Author's collection.*

earlier. Locals shouted their approval throughout the city plaza. Professional baseball had finally arrived in Paris.

When the remaining Students got off the train in Paris, little in the way of a ballpark lay in wait. The team used a small amateur and semipro field north of the cotton compress and Texas and Pacific Depot. In spite of the substandard facility, though, Paris citizens historically turned out for quality baseball, so officials confidently predicted the franchise would succeed in its new home. Without a grandstand, spectators paid a twenty-five-cent entry fee and crowded the foul lines to cheer on the Paris nine. Soon, stalwarts like the bellow-voiced "Rooter" Jackson, a nine-inning annoyance to other fans, assured the team a regular following. Jackson aside, though, Paris baseball had no bigger fan than George Thebo, a local businessman who had introduced the sport to Lamar County three decades earlier.

CHAPTER 7

PARIS: STEPPING UP TO SAVE THE CIRCUIT

George Seth Thebo arrived in Lamar County in 1868, an immigrant from Sandwich, Ontario, Canada, by way of Missouri. The son of French Canadian parents who Anglicized their surname from "Thibault," George left Canada in 1861, presumably traveling down the Ohio and Mississippi Rivers to St. Louis. There, he struck up a romance with Mary LaGrave, also of French descent and a member of the prominent Chateau family, instrumental in the founding of St. Louis. Their common heritage met the approval of Mary's family, and the couple soon married. The LaGrave family was less enthused when Mary announced a pending move to the fledgling agricultural settlement of Paris, Texas, where George's brother Charles experienced surprising success in the Red River Valley real estate business.

After traveling down the Mississippi, the trip through the swampy wild terrain of Louisiana did little to prepare the Thebos for the Lamar County landscape. The Northeast Texas soil, where broken by plow, stuck to a man's boots as a thick, black paste when wet but contracted and cracked like a shattered pane of glass when dry. Like Grayson County, tall-grass prairie swept most of the countryside, a cornucopia of hundreds of plant species with deep roots fed by a seemingly limitless supply of groundwater. Centuries of wildfires filled the soil with untapped nutrients, giving rise to robust harvests of any crop farmers planted. Yet farming did not run in George and Mary Thebo's bloodlines.

Although small in stature, twenty-one-year-old George Thebo quickly developed a reputation as an energetic and enterprising young man. The well-dressed Canadian peddled products throughout Paris from the horse and carriage he housed in the stable behind the Thebo Clarksville Street home. The lavish, two-story home housed the entire Thebo family, including Charles, his wife and their children. On Sundays, the Thebo home attracted Paris's small Catholic population, serving as a makeshift church until a formal building could be built.

While George Thebo brought a knack for business and a religious devotion with him from St. Louis, another passion simmered in his blood—the still-young game of "base ball." George had discovered the game in Missouri when returning Civil War veterans organized local teams and continued playing the sport learned in military camps during the war. With George's influence, Paris would not miss out on the still trendy but growing form of recreation.

Settlers arrived in Lamar County in the early 1820s, but the Texas Congress did not designate the area a county until 1845. Paris, geographically centered between the Red River to the north and Sulphur River to the south, initially served as a small outpost along the northern stretch of Texas's Central National Road. By the Civil War, Lamar County residents named the city the county seat and learned to tap local resources, setting the stage for the area to become the agricultural center of rural Northeast Texas.

During Reconstruction, Paris and Lamar County continued to grow, if only gradually. Unlike Dallas, Fort Worth and, to a certain extent, Sherman and Denison, Paris found difficulty establishing itself commercially. Subsistence farming dampened the need for commerce, but as the area developed, demand for wares increased, and diverse businesses emerged. Paris's city plaza soon became the trading center of Lamar County.

The Texas and Pacific Railroad, building from Sherman toward Texarkana, assured Paris a terminal but not before forcing the city to endure a four-year delay when construction stalled at Brookston, just seven miles west. When the railroad finally did arrive, agriculture quickly transformed from subsistence to a commercial endeavor. Just as the transition began, though, the first of several great Paris fires devastated the fledgling business district. Undeterred, residents quickly rebuilt their community. The Texas and Pacific depot on the southern edge of town became a new center of activity, and a huge compress baled cotton nearby. A cotton oil plant and lumber mill soon followed, supplying manufacturing jobs and steady wages to feed the economy while the rest of the city regained its footing.

By the mid-1880s, one-fourth of Lamar County's twenty thousand residents lived in Paris. Survival still depended on hard work, but locals yearned for amusements to occupy the little leisure time life offered. The back streets around the city plaza offered seedy entertainment but with little of the violence and lawlessness plaguing Denison. Regardless, Paris's entertainment options disturbed George Thebo. As a leader of the local Catholic parish, he couldn't tolerate immorality, especially when it occurred just a few blocks west of his home. Not one to sit idly, instead of lamenting Paris's failings, George took the initiative to do something about it. The game he learned in St. Louis seemed just the cure for the city's ills.

George Thebo fueled baseball's growth as a popular alternative to less wholesome forms of recreation, and local interest in the game must have pleased him. Boys visited the diamond on a regular basis, and their interest soon poured onto the schoolyard, where they played their own version of the game. Even ladies roamed among the spectators. Thebo watched as baseball's local popularity grew, keeping his eye on the game's activity on a national level as well. Like Ted Sullivan, George Thebo believed Texas to be primed for professional baseball, but he realized Paris and similar-sized cities were years from being able to support their own teams. Still, George's efforts bred success, growing his stature as a businessman as well as his influence on community culture.

In spite of George Thebo's passion for baseball, his wife, Mary, held contempt for the game. Like many of the nineteenth century, Mary thought idleness synonymous with laziness. Baseball offered little more than an excuse for loafing, and as a profession—well, only a vagrant would even consider being paid to play a game. She made it very clear that her children would have nothing to do with baseball. George, on the other hand, quietly held out hope.

By 1884, George Thebo was father to seven-year-old Mary Ann and an exceptionally quick three-year-old son, Tony. George continued working to expand his business interests, selling insurance and extending his merchant operations into Indian Territory. In his spare time, though, George enjoyed watching the Quicksteps, Paris's first semiprofessional baseball team. The Quicksteps benefited from an association with Paris's cottonseed oil mill, established by future plaza fountain donor J.J. Culbertson. The team played on a diamond on the oil mill property, and when mill business was strong, players might pick up a small payment for their efforts on the field. Paris's semiprofessional team did not rival those of the railroad teams in Grayson County, but it offered the city a first taste of organized ball.

Pitcher and seventeen-year-old Paris native Bobby Walker led the Quicksteps. A lanky youngster with a streaking fastball, the gloveless Walker became well known among other North Texas semipro clubs, who clamored for a chance to face the young pitcher. In the summer of 1884, the Dallas Brown Stockings called Bobby and his Quicksteps teammates west for a three-game series. The Brown Stockings, one of Texas's most successful semipro teams, had no intention of being shown up in their own park and secured the services of a professional pitcher for the series. Regardless, Paris played respectably, even winning one of the three games decisively, 20–9.

The Quicksteps' reputation as a crack nine bred an intense rivalry with the Sliders, another semipro team based in Bonham, thirty miles west of Paris along the Texas and Pacific Railroad. The teams faced each other frequently in front of large crowds, the most dedicated fans traveling with their teams to the opposing city. A few miles east of Paris, Blossom Prairie's aggregation offered regular competition as well, fielding a uniquely barefooted team with blazing speed. Baseball equipment, even rudimentary gloves or footwear lighter than leather boots, had yet to make its way to the Paris area.

Whatever the Quicksteps might have lacked in defense, they made up for at the plate and on the bases. In July 1884, Paris spotted a lesser opponent ten runs but still managed to pull out a 31–29 victory. Not an uncommonly high-scoring affair for the time, the Quicksteps thirty-four fielding errors made for a memorable game. Their opponents, though falling short on the scoreboard, found greater success in the field, posting a mere thirty-two errors, surely aided by their familiarity with the pasture they called home field.

While Paris flirted with semiprofessional baseball, the city's infrastructure continued to grow. In the early 1890s, attention focused on construction of a courthouse, eventually finished in 1895. Paris had become an increasingly important city, and smaller communities like Petty, Roxton, Maxey and Blossom came to rely on the services offered by the county seat. Urban areas to the west could not ignore Lamar County's growing impact on North Texas. Unfortunately, an incident in 1893 painted a poor picture of Paris throughout the entire country, if not the world.

Like those in Grayson County, Lamar County residents had voted against secession. Though few in the county owned slaves, racism was a societal norm. Like most in the South, locals considered African Americans citizens only to the extent federal law required, and Parisians happily took advantage of their cheap labor. One such African American was Henry Smith, an on-and-off employee of several local residents and an acquaintance of police officer and jailer Henry Vance.

Vance and Smith had a contentious relationship. Vance had arrested Smith, a noted drunk and public nuisance, on more than one occasion, and at some point the two had an altercation in the jail. Smith vowed to gain revenge on Vance, claiming Vance had unfairly beaten him. One afternoon while Vance left for work at the jail, his three-year-old daughter, Myrtle, played in the front yard of their Lamar Street home. Henry Vance never saw his daughter alive again.

The aftermath of Myrtle Vance's murder is well documented. Captured a few days later in Arkansas, Henry Smith confessed to the crime and arrived by train a day later in Lamar County. A mob of thousands swarmed the shackled man when he stepped off the train at the Texas and Pacific depot. Law enforcement offered no resistance as the crowd seized Smith and paraded him through the streets to the plaza and back to a pasture near the depot, a short distance from the baseball diamond. There, Parisians dished out their own form of justice, tying Smith atop a wooden scaffold and torturing him with white-hot steel rods for nearly an hour. The event ended in an inferno, with the scaffold and Smith both set ablaze. At the end of the day, the charred remains of Henry Smith became fodder for souvenir hunters, and within the week, reporters from as far as New York descended on Paris. The ridicule brought on the city by the Henry Smith episode lingered for many years and remains a point of embarrassment to this day.

Devout Catholics and Canadian natives, George and Mary Thebo detested racism and confined their family to the house in the days leading up to Henry Smith's lynching. Thebo was indeed a gentle man and raised his family accordingly. Undoubtedly, Tony, thirteen years old at the time, would have loved to follow his friends to the biggest event Parisians ever witnessed, but he knew better. The Thebo children later described the days surrounding the lynching as scary and horrific. George and Tony undoubtedly thought of the incident on future trips to the baseball grounds, where the aura of death lingered in the air.

By the mid-1890s, on a much improved ball field, George Thebo watched as fellow Canadian Russ Steinhoff, released from Denison's 1896 entry into the Texas League, managed Paris's latest semipro team. Tony Thebo, by then a teenager, had taken up baseball to the dismay of his mother and, when not attending the games, could be found with Ben Shelton, an exceptional local ballplayer a few years his senior. Tony quickly developed his own reputation, and locals looked forward to the day his gazelle-like speed would grace the Paris base paths. If Tony had his way, that day would come soon.

Although baseball offered both the players and spectators a popular diversion, even George Thebo would admit the game's local growth was but a footnote to Paris's growth as a railroad town. By the end of the 1880s, both the Santa Fe and Frisco joined the Texas and Pacific in serving Paris, and both travelers and freight arrived in the city from all directions. Just as importantly, Parisians could travel away from town with relative ease and convenience. Like every other city in North Texas, the railroads would have a great impact on Paris's early forays into professional baseball.

When the Sherman tornado struck in the spring of 1896, Paris was busily recovering from a disaster of its own—another of the fires that plagued the business district. As citizens scrambled to rebuild their businesses and homes, the cotton industry on the southern edge of Paris once again kept the community economically viable. The railroads provided a sufficient supply of goods, and steamboats along the Red River twelve miles to the north transported what rail traffic could not. Soon, the American flag once again flew proudly over the city plaza, where bankers, merchants and no fewer than five saloons served Lamar County. With a partially paved street system, ornate Victorian houses and reliable streetcar service for a nickel's fare, Paris forged toward the twentieth century.

Keeping shop on the plaza at that time were two druggists, with physicians' offices occupying their upper floors. One office held the practice of one-time Paris Quicksteps hurler Bobby Walker, known locally as Dr. Robert R. Walker. Having remained involved in local baseball and a prominent citizen, Texas League president John Ward didn't hesitate to call on Walker to head up the Paris franchise's business operations. Walker's first move was to sign Russ Steinhoff as field manager.

Former big leaguer Billy Crowell, Sherman's Wirt Spencer and Grayson County's Cy Mulkey anchored Paris's pitching staff. Dutch Herold, the well-traveled A.C. Jantzen, Steinhoff, William Van Dresser and Dit Spencer made up the infield, while the outfield included future dentist Dudley Payne, William Cathey and right fielder Bill Zeis. Although Steinhoff managed the club and knew the strategic aspects of baseball, it wasn't long until his miserable fielding cost him his release. Walker promoted catcher A.C. Jantzen to his position.

As Paris prepared for its first game, a summer remembered for its searing heat arrived in North Texas. The team took the field for the first time on June 14 in Dallas, with the temperature at ninety degrees. It would be the coolest day Paris players would enjoy for the remainder of the season. Daily highs rose and remained at or near one hundred degrees the rest of the summer, with little wind and scant rainfall. Games normally started at 3:00 p.m., with players and spectators alike forced to endure the hottest part of the day. Unfortunately, for most of the season, the scoreboard offered Paris little in the way of relief.

In the franchise opener, Paris fell to the Dallas Navigators by a score of 9–5. Billy Crowell pitched a complete game, something expected of most pitchers at the time, giving up twelve hits and four walks. Its first game in the books, Paris followed with another loss to Dallas and a humiliating 14–1 defeat at the hands of Fort Worth. As Paris readied for a June 17 game at the Fort Worth Panthers' home stadium, fans still awaited word of their team's first victory.

Although Billy Crowell gave up seventeen hits, including a home run, the Panthers managed to score only three earned runs on visiting Paris. Still, with five unearned runs on two Paris errors, Fort Worth had taken an 8–7 lead by the end of the fifth inning. From that point on, Crowell shut down the Panthers. Paris tied the game in the seventh, and Crowell led them to a twelve-inning, 9–8 victory, the first in Paris franchise history. Paris lost the remaining two games of the series before returning home to host the Galveston Sand Crabs with only one win to its credit.

Billy Crowell again took the mound against Galveston, scattering nine hits in a 6–5 win elating a home crowd said to number in the hundreds. A.C. Jantzen hit Paris's first home run on its own diamond, adding a triple and scoring two runs. According to the *Dallas Morning News*, Grayson County's Bee Spencer was sensational in the field. The following day, Cy Mulkey followed with another outstanding appearance on the mound and went three for five in a 5–2 victory.

Paris continued play through the end of June, when they put together a five-game winning streak at home against Houston, Austin and Denison. A.C. Jantzen led the team in hitting, stealing bases and pounding out base hits and home runs on a daily basis, while Billy Crowell and Cy Mulkey continued to offer effective pitching. With Sherman's wins and losses inherited as part of its official record, Paris closed the first segment of the season in third place with a 34-35 record.

The second segment of the 1896 season began on Independence Day in Denison, where the Tigers swept Paris in a three-game series. The team then headed on its first southern road trip, eventually stumbling home with a 4-9 record, new uniforms and a new official name, the Texas Midlands, honoring the railroad extending its line from Cooper to Paris a few years earlier. The new identity and friendly fans sparked the Midlands to win five of six games, including consecutive victories of 21–7 and 18–8 over Dallas. During the two games, Paris collected a total of thirty-nine hits, including eight by recently signed outfielder George Nie.

A week later after dominating the Navigators at home, the Midlands headed for Dallas for a two-game series. Billy Crowell, George Nie and other players chatted with passengers or read Sandy Neville's account of the previous game in the *Paris News* as the train made stops at Santa Fe depots in Roxton, Ben Franklin and Pecan Gap. When they arrived in Ladonia, though, railroad officials handed A.C. Jantzen a wire from Dallas. The Dallas Navigators had disbanded, and the Midlands would have no opponent upon arrival. Before the return train reached Paris, Denison announced it would cease operations as well, leaving Paris and Fort Worth as the only stops on the northern swing of the Texas League. Shermanites, still stinging from the *Denison Daily*'s jabs at the city in its time of need, likely celebrated the Denison club's demise.

Within a day of the departure of Dallas and Denison from the league, South Texas team officials concluded that the jump from Fort Worth to Paris would be too costly. Galveston threatened to withdraw from the league unless the Paris franchise relocated closer to Fort Worth. On July 31, at a league meeting in Houston, the remaining owners decided to transfer the team to Dallas in order to save the remainder of the season. President Ward expected Paris supporters to fight for their team, but on August 2, under sunny skies and a high temperature of 107 degrees, the Texas Midlands played their last game of 1896, a 15–8 loss at the hands of the Fort Worth Panthers. The franchise then relocated for the second time in the season, finishing the second half with a 10-14 record, good for only seventh place in the eight-team league.

Paris completed its first season of professional baseball with a 19-25 record after relocating from Sherman. Billy Crowell led the team with thirteen wins, while A.C. Jantzen hit eleven home runs and Billy Oswald gained ninety-five hits. Tom Menefee, although having played only a few games with Paris, hit .340 on the season as he split time with the Austin Senators franchise. Despite its team's early exit from the league, professional baseball had taken hold in Paris, and by the end of the 1896 season, officials planned to secure a franchise for the following season. George Thebo settled into his increasingly successful insurance business and awaited a second year of professional baseball.

CHAPTER 8

1897: THE INCREASING RAILROAD INFLUENCE

Ned Green should have lived a charmed life. Born in London in 1867 to millionaire silk trader Edward Green, Ned's parents were among the wealthiest Americans living overseas. Aside from his father's fortune, Ned's mother inherited several million dollars from her family's New England whaling fleet after her father's death a few years earlier. The Greens' combined wealth and the income it generated could have sustained a family for generations.

Outwardly, the Greens appeared to be a happy family, but financial tension strained the marriage. Her fortune dwarfing that of her husband, Mrs. Green demanded Edward sign a prenuptial agreement. Soon, accusations of forgery involving the will of Mrs. Green's aunt forced the couple to flee the country for London, where their wealth continued to grow. Mrs. Green's harsh upbringing as a New England Quaker continued to fuel the family tension. Despite her wealth, Ned's mother exhibited conservatism far in excess of the Quaker spirit, going so far as to send young Ned from their lavish apartment into the filthy London streets to resell the morning's newspaper after she had read it.

By 1875, when the statute of limitations on forgery expired, the Greens returned to the United States, settling in Bellows Falls, Vermont, a six-hour train ride from New York City. While in Bellows Falls, Edward Green made a series of bad investments and watched his bankroll dwindle. By 1881, Green lost his entire fortune. He soon lost his family as well, his wife implementing her rights under the prenuptial agreement and moving Ned, his younger sister and her money to New York City.

In New York, Mrs. Green became a Wall Street sensation, building a fortune unheard of for a female in the investment world, mainly through trading railroad stocks and mortgages. Her wealth dwarfing their own, ailing companies and even the New York City government called on Mrs. Green for bailouts. She often obliged, but she was not quick to shower her wealth upon her family. Hetty Howland Robinson Green was, unfortunately for Ned and his sister, the infamous "Witch of Wall Street," a notorious accumulator of wealth who forced her family to live in squalor.

Flamboyant northerner Edward Howland Robinson Green brought both his railroad and interest in baseball to Paris. *Author's collection.*

Hetty Green had sealed her reputation as a miser long before moving to New York. When nine-year-old Ned suffered a dislocated kneecap while sledding in Vermont, his mother saved the doctor's fee and treated the injury herself despite a complete ignorance of medicine. When the injury later became debilitating, she and Ned visited a charity clinic disguised as paupers. The doctor recognized the multimillionaire and demanded payment, enraging Hetty Green to the point that she took Ned home without treatment. Ned continued to live with his severe and painful injury until his teens, when a case of gangrene forced the amputation of his leg, which was buried on his parents' Bellows Falls property.

In New York, Hetty's conservative lifestyle became legendary. Always dressed in black, she refused to heat her home or use hot water and ate fifteen-cent pies or oatmeal daily. Unwilling to rent an office, she worked from any bank's empty desk and became convinced that she was the target of assassins. Hetty made every effort to instill the same paranoia in Ned.

After Ned graduated from Fordham University and obtained his law license, his mother sent him to Chicago to manage her Midwest financial affairs. As Hetty Green moved from apartment to apartment to avoid establishing a residence and being liable for taxes, she paid Ned little, forcing him to live as cheaply as he had been raised. Ned obliged, and as soon as he proved his ability and loyalty, Hetty sent him to rural Texas to manage her interests in a small railroad acquired through foreclosure.

Like so many other North Texas towns, Terrell was built by the railroad. The community sprung up in 1873 around a one-hundred-acre lot donated for construction of a Texas and Pacific depot. Within two years, Terrell's population reached over one thousand, and by 1885, it had become a full-blown commercial center. The same year, state officials picked Terrell as home of the North Texas Insane Asylum, delivering jobs, increasing the population and leading the city into an era of manufacturing and transportation.

The Houston and Texas Central Railroad originally planned to extend service through the Terrell area to Paris in the early 1880s. Though planning to connect with the Frisco Railroad approaching from the north, by 1892, the HTC branch lay incomplete. The line's investors in bankruptcy, Hetty Green assumed control. She appointed Ned, now known by his full name, Edward Howland Robinson (E.H.R.) Green, as president and general manager of the Texas Midland Railroad, its headquarters in Terrell.

Ned soon engaged in expanding and improving the Texas Midland, even installing electric lights in coach cars, the first of their kind in Texas. The investment surely angered his mother. After all, Hetty Green's interests lay in profits, not customer service. The railroad became lavishly successful, however, so she could find little fault in her son's decisions. Had she known of his philanthropy in outfitting the local baseball team and financing a community brass band, she would have thought quite differently.

E.H.R. Green became a stalwart in Texas as both an influential Republican and businessman. Much to his mother's chagrin, Green also became a well-known free spender. He enjoyed the high life, taking in a former prostitute from Chicago as a permanent companion and hosting lavish parties at his Terrell home.

Despite his business success, Ned's true interest lay in his hobbies. He purchased stamps and coins in large quantities, eventually assembling the world's most valuable stamp collection. Soon an internationally known philatelist and numismatist, Ned's reputation could not have been more

The Texas Midland Railroad made several stops along its route from Ennis to Paris, including one at this depot in Kaufman County's Rosser. *Karen Rutherford photo.*

DAY 1 2 3 4 5 6 7 8 9 10 11 12 13 14 15 16 17 18 19 20 21

JAN FEB MAR APR MAY JUN JUL AUG SEP OCT NOV DEC 31 30 29 28 27 26 25 24 23 22

Texas & Pacific R'y.

1898
1899
1900
1901
1902

Account of PARIS TRANSFER CO.

Good for Transfer of One Passenger with Ordinary Baggage,
From Texas & Pacific Railway Depot
At PARIS, Tex.
To Depot indicated by Punch Mark in margin.

G. C. & S. F.	★
St. L. & S. F.	★
TEX. MID.	★
IF ½ TICKET PUNCH HERE	★

This Ticket expires on date punched in margin hereof, after which date or if more than one date is cancelled, it is void, and will not be accepted for passage.

3121 Form P. T.

Gen'l Pass. & Ticket Agent.

A ballplayer traveling via the Texas and Pacific Railroad through Paris would have used a ticket like this to make a railroad transfer in the late 1800s. *Courtesy AntiqueMystique.com.*

opposite that of his mother's, and he reveled in the public attention. The Texas press delighted in reporting Ned's chauffeured automobile trip from Terrell to Dallas, a trip representing Texas's first travel by horseless carriage—and also first traffic accident, as a team of horses forced Green's vehicle off the road.

By 1895, the Texas Midland Railroad's success begged for expansion. With the Frisco providing Paris service from points northward, Green planned a southern route, first extending his railroad to Commerce, the new home of East Texas Normal College. A few miles northeast, Delta County seat Cooper gained a stop along the rail line as well, and ultimately the Texas Midland completed its connection through Enloe to Paris.

Ned Green's popularity soared as the Texas Midland route became a lifeline for Lamar County. Officials at Grove, a small settlement southwest of Paris, renamed their community Howland in honor of the tycoon. More honors followed, and after 1911, Texas governor Oscar Branch Colquitt bestowed Green the rank of colonel, a title he proudly flaunted the rest of his life.

Ned Green knew marketing, and he promoted Paris as the railroad center it eventually became. Ideally situated as a northern route between Dallas and Texarkana, and with several rail companies having converged on the city, Green foresaw Paris's growth and considered moving the Texas Midland headquarters to the town. He ultimately continued the operation in Terrell, but Green had other plans for Paris. His brief involvement with Terrell's baseball team planted a seed of interest in the sport, and with money to help it grow, Ned sought to invest in baseball as a business proposition.

When discussions of a new Texas League season began in late 1896, Green quickly enlisted Paris residents Augustine H. O'Neill and A.W. "Sandy" Neville to represent his interests. O'Neill, a community leader and manager of Paris's cotton compress, and Neville, a local newspaper publisher, teamed with attorney Jim Patrick to negotiate a second franchise for Paris. In March 1897, Patrick and Neville traveled to the Texas League meeting in Fort Worth, presenting their case for a team against contingents from Shreveport, New Orleans and Sherman-Denison.

Outclassed in market size, Patrick and Neville first argued Paris deserved a franchise after saving the Sherman team on short notice the previous year. League officials offered little support, countering that the Paris team did not even complete the partial season it inherited. With prospects for a new team bleak and attention turning to the Louisiana representatives, Patrick reached into his wallet and retrieved a cashier's check in the amount of $2,500, a guarantee to support the team for an entire season. Neither New Orleans nor Shreveport offered such assurances, and league officials accepted Paris's offer without further discussion. Fortunately for Jim Patrick, they took the guarantee on his word and did not accept his check. It wasn't even certified.

While Paris lobbied for its spot in the Texas League, Sherman and Denison representatives did the same. South Texas owners didn't support franchises in North Texas's small cities, noting that the locations made for awkward jumps and provided gate receipts well below those of larger cities. But with Dallas and Fort Worth secure, North Texas needed two franchises to ensure a balanced league and affordable road trips. Sherman and Denison, both having tried and failed to field teams separately, buried the hatchet long enough to form an association represented by fellow Confederate veterans Leonidas Maughs and Will Batsell. Like Patrick and Neville, Maughs and Batsell attended the Fort Worth meeting, and when the two prospective Louisiana cities hesitated, they rode Paris's coattails, proposing a joint team splitting home games between the two cities. With railroad support in place, and a relatively short jump to Paris, the league accepted the proposal, setting the slate of teams for 1897.

Maughs and Batsell hired Mobile manager Pete Weckbecker to head the Sherman-Denison franchise. Weckbecker, a veteran of the Virginia League and a former major leaguer, set to work organizing in each community, selling a limited number of season tickets and making arrangements for concessions and scorecards. More importantly, he planned to refurbish the Denison playing field, considered the worst in the league in 1896. In fact, upon inspecting the infield, Weckbecker discovered the pitcher's box to be nearly ten feet farther from home plate than the sixty feet, four inches stated in the rulebook.

Weckbecker assembled a team anchored by pitchers James McGinnis and Frank Quigg, along with barehanded first baseman Bill Kemmer and utility infielder Joe Dowie. Heavy-hitting Pearce "No Use" Chiles led the outfield. Chiles, a future major leaguer, earned his nickname via his boisterous shouts of "It's no use!" whenever a hitter struck the ball in his direction. His bark, however, was far louder than his bite, as Chiles amassed no small number of errors over the course of his career. What Chiles couldn't achieve within the rules, he accomplished illegally. He developed an elaborate method of stealing signals as a catcher, an accomplice with binoculars shocking Chiles as notification via a buried electrical wire Chiles stuffed in his shoe at the beginning of each inning.

Weckbecker took a heavy risk in signing Chiles, who had spent most of the 1896 season running from a charge of rape and offered Weckbecker no guarantee that he'd stay out of jail long enough to reach Grayson County. The rape charge didn't stick, but Chiles's luck ran out four years later when officials arrested him for his part in an El Paso con game. Sentenced to two years in Huntsville prison, Chiles proved as devious as he had on the baseball field, escaping within a year and disappearing for good. For 1897, though, Chiles's seemingly split personality perfectly matched Weckbecker's geographically split team. With a new infield, bleachers, souvenirs and special railroad fares between Sherman and Denison set by early April, both Grayson County and Weckbecker awaited the Sherman-Denison Tigers opening game against Paris on April 17.

While Pete Weckbecker brought a wealth of baseball experience to the Texas League, Paris business manager Sandy Neville described himself as only a casual fan. Accepting his position out of civic interest and the fact that "there was work to be done," Neville assembled his own team, supported wholeheartedly with E.H.R. Green's vast fortune. Neville resigned the notoriously powerful but painfully slow A.C. Jantzen as manager along with former Austin shortstop Bobby Burns and new Texas Leaguer Dan Boland. Second baseman Elmo Jacobs and future major-league third baseman Jake Thielmann rounded out the infield. The outfield changed frequently throughout the season, as most players rotated between positions, but George Nie appeared most steadily.

Ed Dillon, Charles Noland and Irwin Isaacs made up the Midlands pitching staff, with Chicago's W.W. Beckwith a late season acquisition. An employee of E.H.R. Green at the Atlas Gumbo Plant south of Paris, Beckwith appeared in Sandy Neville's office one afternoon, introducing himself as a ballplayer. Suitably impressed after a tryout, Neville signed Beckwith to a contract, and he remained with the team for the rest of the season. But Beckwith didn't gain his true fame on the baseball diamond. He later returned to the upper Midwest, where he married Abraham Lincoln's granddaughter and fathered the last direct descendant of the former president. Eventually the couple divorced, much to the delight of the disapproving Lincoln family. Ned Green would have applauded Beckwith's willingness to take a stand against a family nearly as powerful as his own.

The Texas Midlands baseball club of 1897 opened at Denison in front of one thousand spectators and proceeded to play dismally, losing eleven of its first fourteen games. A.C. Jantzen filled the one bright spot in the lineup, pounding out base hits seemingly at will for the second straight year. The pitching staff performed less admirably, allowing seven runs per game, backed by a completely inept defense.

Buried in last place by the end of April and with forty-two team errors already to its credit, the Midlands opened May with a road trip to Fort Worth, followed by a tour of the league's southern cities. Losing fourteen consecutive games and being spared a possible fifteenth by a rainout in Houston, the Midlands surrendered nearly ten runs per game during the trip. Insisting his team would improve regardless of cost, Ned Green moved into the shadows and left the team in the hands of Sandy Neville. After all, E.H.R. Green was not one to associate closely with failing operations. Then again, he was not one to admit defeat and vowed to continue financial support.

The home diamond offered the travel-weary Midlands relief, which translated into success on the scoreboard. They finished May with a 7-6 record, scoring ten runs per game behind blistering hot batting. Not all victories had to be earned, however, as the Midlands' success was aided by a 9–0 forfeit by Austin on May 17 when the Senators refused to take the field following a disagreement with the umpire with the score tied in extra-innings. It was the first of five games on Paris's schedule ending in a forfeit, the Midlands on the winning side of three.

When June arrived, Paris lingered in last place with a 12-31 record, fourteen games behind league leader San Antonio and nine games behind next-to-last-place Dallas. The Midlands won five of their next nine, but a mid-June six-game losing streak sealed another unsuccessful month. Mercifully, the first half of the Texas League season ended on June 27 with Paris holding a 21-48 record, still seven games behind Dallas and twenty-five behind first-half champion San Antonio. Even Charles Noland's pet possum, the team's newfound mascot, couldn't bring the Midlands luck on the field as the pitching staff continued allowing ten-run games on a regular basis with the infield's bumbling lack of support.

While the Midlands struggled through the season's first half, Weckbecker's Sherman-Denison Tigers remained competitive. Beginning the season with a four-game winning streak, the Tigers essentially split the remainder of their games, ending the first half with a 35-35 record. Weckbecker's off-field antics, though, overshadowed the Tigers' accomplishments, and the results deepened the Sherman-Denison divide.

During the season's first month, Sherman-Denison played eleven home games, five at Sherman's Batsell's Park and six in Denison. The arrangement seemed to be working out well. Games attracted a steady stream of spectators, and both streetcar systems and the railroad connecting the two cities profited. Weckbecker, though, found the arrangement far from satisfying. Denison baseball representatives, he claimed, paid his full contracted salary, and he expected the Sherman delegation to come up with its agreed upon share. Sherman, however, refused. If Leonidas Maughs and Denison wanted to assume payment of Weckbecker's full contract, it was their choice. Sherman denied any obligation to see Weckbecker's salary increased by paying him in excess of what his contract specified.

Sherman's refusal to effectively increase Weckbecker's salary incensed the manager. Before the May 23 game against Houston, he ordered each player to rip the "S" from his uniform and declared the team's association with Sherman void. Despite Sherman's protests, Weckbecker didn't back down, and apparently Leonidas Maughs did not pressure him. Perhaps the shouts of foul play from Sherman were too much, however, because within two weeks, Weckbecker left the team, replaced by "No Use" Chiles.

Denison's .500 first-half winning percentage was good for fifth place in the league. Opening the second half with two wins in Fort Worth and five straight in Dallas and Paris, the Tigers appeared ready to make a run at the second-half pennant. But on June 12, the team abruptly announced it was leaving Denison for Waco, claiming poor local attendance and financial losses on southern road trips. The shift to Waco, it expected, would improve the Tigers' financial standing both in terms of home attendance and decreased travel costs.

While Pete Weckbecker did nothing to endear himself to the Grayson County fans, and Pearce Chiles's reputation likely drove others from the grandstands, grumbling Texas League officials blamed local baseball "kranks." No franchise could survive without meeting its guarantee of $50 to the visiting team, and if locals wanted professional baseball, they needed to put up their money. In fact, though, the Tigers put up a bit too much money. Despite the league salary cap, Denison's monthly payroll exceeded the league's average by $200, an impossible expense for one of the two smallest markets. So the Tigers took their high payroll south to Waco, finishing the season with a 19-17 record (63-57 overall), good for second place in the league but well behind pennant-winning Galveston.

With Denison out of the league and Paris the lone remaining small-city franchise, E.H.R. Green wasted no time pronouncing his continued financial support. The season's second half brought minor roster changes but far fewer than needed to alter the Texas Midlands' fortunes. The Midlands released

Despite running afoul of John McCloskey, Jake Thielmann went on to a long Major League career. *Author's collection.*

Irwin Isaacs and former big-league pitcher Ed Pabst, who refused a twenty-five dollar pay cut. Lem Bailey arrived from Evansville in an effort to bolster the pitching staff, and Sandy Neville traded Ed Dillon for the superstitious Mikey "Sky High" Hobright, who had recently fallen out of favor with Dallas manager John McCloskey. In fact, "fallen out of favor" is a bit of an understatement. When Hobright questioned McCloskey's authority between innings, the old Texas Leaguer cold-cocked him and offered his release. McCloskey did not reserve his antics for Hobright, though. Jake Thielmann had his own run-in with McCloskey a year or two later when the manager again lost his temper and beat Thielmann in the dugout. Ever the peacemaker, Jake accepted responsibility for the episode and pointed out McCloskey as an upstanding fellow who carried him to the best doctor in town after the game. Perhaps McCloskey believed his work in founding the Texas League a decade earlier deserved more respect than his players offered.

The Midlands' second half began ominously at Dallas on June 28. The Paris franchise, now dubbed by newspaper reporters as the "Parisians," "Frenchmen" and "Frog Eaters," fell behind 10–0 after four innings. With rain on the horizon and the game not yet official, the Midlands attempted to stall in hopes of a rainout. Pitchers began lobbing the ball to the plate, and the oblivious Dallas batters gleefully pounded it around the diamond, where the Paris fielders refused to make plays. Soon, the rain began, and the Midlands thought they had pulled a coup. The umpire, however, felt differently and awarded Dallas a 10–0 win. The outwitted Midlands went on to lose six of the next seven before returning home to play the league's southern teams. In a summer when the Paris temperature topped one hundred degrees twenty-six times, the Midlands spent the remainder of the season hoping for the relief rain might bring and maybe a chance to try the stunt of June 28 a second time.

Paris had its most successful run of the season in mid-July, posting a 10-6 record, including winning two of three games against Austin, San Antonio and Houston. Lem Bailey and James Callahan pitched well, the only exception being when Bailey opened a 6–5 loss to Houston by walking three, hitting one and committing an error. The Midlands followed up the defeat with a 20–0 victory over the Buffalos the next day, the most lopsided win Paris fans would see in the city's years in the Texas League. Paris played a rare errorless game, smashing out twenty-one hits, nine for extra bases. Houston's poor fielding contributed to Paris's success, as the Buffalos committed seven errors and surrendered sixteen unearned runs. The umpire called the lopsided contest after just five innings. After all, had the game continued, it might have taken over two hours to play, an exceedingly long contest for the time.

The victory over Houston represented one of three Paris shutouts on the season, the other two forfeits including a game against Fort Worth when a Panther player threw his bat at umpire James Callahan, a Paris pitcher who had been enlisted to officiate in the absence of a league umpire. After being ejected, the batter accused Callahan of favoring the Midlands and refused to leave the field. Backed by his teammates, who agreed before the game that Callahan would be an impartial judge, he continued his verbal assault on the umpire. Ultimately, the delay forced Callahan to award Paris a 9–0 decision.

At the end of July, Paris still found itself in last place with a 12-21 record, nine games out of first place. After the Midlands surrendered fourteen runs to Galveston in consecutive games, rumors that the team would be dropped from the league began to spread. For the second year in a row, Paris's distance from the other North Texas teams threatened to cost the city its baseball club.

Dallas manager John McCloskey suggested Paris relocate to Corsicana to reduce travel expenses for all of the league's franchises; however, he clearly underestimated the resources of E.H.R. Green. Green insisted the Midlands continue play, even offering to pay the expenses of visiting clubs. Attendance remained steady with gimmicks like a balloon liftoff scheduled in order to draw spectators to the ballpark. Although several players left the Midlands to join clubs in the Arkansas League, Paris remained in the league through season's end, finishing the second half with a 20-33 record after dropping five of the last eight games to Waco, the relocated Sherman-Denison franchise.

The *Dallas Morning News* perhaps described the Texas Midlands season of 1897 best, summarizing it in a single paragraph ironically written after the home opener, a 13–3 loss at the hands of Sherman-Denison in which the Midlands committed eight errors:

> *The Midlands played a decidedly rotten game from start to finish and were clearly outclassed... The Midlands lacked energy and apparently took but little interest in the game. They were decidedly slow in all their movements. Their fielding and batting was miserable, and they seldom got their hands on a ball even if it came within reach. It is hoped that no such game will ever be witnessed on the diamond... again.*

With the season concluded, Robert Walker and Sandy Neville became embroiled in a dispute over $625 in player salaries, and in the end, the Midlands franchise paid its bills largely with public donations. Although he later became one of America's greatest philanthropists, on this day, E.H.R. Green proved that his mother had taught him well. When officials negotiated payouts, Ned was nowhere to be found.

CHAPTER 9

1902: THE INTERURBAN AND A TEAM FOR THE AGES

Just days into the 1898 season, the North Texas League folded when Dallas and Fort Worth faced financial difficulties. Soon thereafter, the Spanish-American War dominated the public interest, and baseball took a back seat to national security. The Texas League's southern teams continued playing through the war years, but Dallas and Fort Worth couldn't find financial backing, and the southern owners remained leery of North Texas's small cities. Although some individual or group flirted with starting a new North Texas circuit each year, nothing came of their efforts. It was 1902 before interest returned, and organizers of the North Texas League soon learned that much had changed during baseball's hiatus.

As the twentieth century approached, Texas railroad construction lagged behind the rest of the country. While rail lines connected most cities and many small towns along the lines prospered, the geographically largest state in the country had only ten thousand miles of track. The railroad had yet to reach the Panhandle, South and West Texas, with travel west of Fort Worth difficult. For cities vying for professional baseball franchises, however, the tracks crisscrossing North, East and Central Texas made for easy travel, and even more improvements lay on the horizon.

James P. Crearer arrived in Denison from Ottawa, Ontario, in 1896. A former college football player and amateur boxer, the muscular forty-year-old left his accounting job at the Bank of Montreal and headed to Texas with plans to enter the railroad business. Unlike other railroad moguls, though, Crearer's interest did not lie in freight-based rail. The transcontinental

The Sherman-Denison Interurban. *Courtesy Grayson County GenWeb.*

railroads' success could not be disputed, but Crearer had neither the finances nor interest to compete with them. On the other hand, street rail had proven lucrative on a local basis. By the mid-1890s, electric streetcar systems had largely replaced the mule-drawn cars, and both George Blackford of Denison and Will Batsell of Sherman had converted their streetcar companies to electrical power. Upon arriving in Grayson County, Crearer marveled at Sherman and Denison's streetcar systems and charted his course for his next endeavor, harnessing the local electric model to connect the two cities, a system he called the "Interurban" rail.

Years before J.P. Crearer arrived in Grayson County, Will Batsell recognized local attractions as key to a street rail system's success. Simply providing transportation throughout the community was not enough. Streetcar companies needed popular destinations to maintain clientele and sustain profits. In 1897, Austin street rail manager J.K. Urie spoke of the importance of recreational attractions in an address to the Texas Street Rail Association. As with any business, he noted, location meant everything. An attraction must be far enough from the city center to make walking inconvenient but close enough to make riding in a crowded streetcar tolerable. Sporting events could be profitable with enough advertising, but true profits required a destination—a recreation site open to visitors on a regular basis. People yearned for leisure activities, particularly on Sundays, the only day many did not have to work. The public held a special interest in water-based recreation like swimming, boating, fishing and lakeside picnicking. Most importantly, though, an attraction had to be sustainable—a place to which visitors would return week after week. Ideally, an attraction would be accessible only by street rail, with all visitors buying a streetcar ticket to gain admittance.

Whether J.K. Urie's presentation influenced J.P. Crearer isn't known, but Crearer soon embarked on an ambitious effort to develop a recreation area along his proposed Interurban line between Sherman and Denison. Choosing a spring-fed site midway between the two cities on the eastern side of his Interurban right of way, Crearer constructed a dam creating a small lake. Woodlake, as it became known, remained a popular recreational destination for nearly a half century, attracting Grayson County residents to its forty-acre park offering water sports, wildlife, pavilions, a casino and other facilities. Crearer based his Interurban operation at Woodlake, with rail-feeding electrical turbines, a car storage area and a maintenance facility all serving the line outside the park's public area. For a fee of twenty-five cents, residents of Sherman and Denison could travel round-trip, park admission included. Crearer's creation provided incentive for locals to travel the Interurban, which made its first run on May 1, 1901. Woodlake soon replaced Sherman's Batsell's Park and Denison's Forest Park as Grayson County's popular recreation area, effectively bringing Sherman and Denison together on neutral ground between the cities. With a popular new park, the Interurban once again encouraged local enthusiasts to bring professional baseball to the area.

While J.P. Crearer placed his hopes for Grayson County in electric-powered transportation, Corsicana's 1894 oil discovery opened untold opportunities for the Navarro County city. Between 1894 and 1900, Corsicana's population doubled to nearly ten thousand, with over three hundred oil wells within the city limits. The oil boom spawned countless local businesses, including a refinery, saloons, retail stores, hotels, banks and a dozen newspapers. Even before the oil discovery, Corsicana served as an important stop on the HTC railroad, with local producers shipping a steady stream of farm products, including cotton, from the area. Local agriculture business owner Doak Roberts had kept farmers supplied with seed, hay and grain since the mid-

1880s, and though not involved in the oil business, he fully recognized what it meant to the Navarro County economy. For Roberts, a booming economy and increasing population offered potential for his favorite pastime—baseball.

Jesse Doak Roberts was born in 1870 in Navarro County, the son of native Arkansan and local politician Hawkins Roberts. The elder Roberts, a Confederate veteran, served as justice of the peace and coroner in Navarro County. Soon after the horrific Paris lynching of 1893, Hawkins Roberts became embroiled in a lynching scandal of his own when he failed to stop and, as some newspapers reported, actually encouraged the lynching of black man accused of rape. In short, Roberts said that the man got what was coming to him. Doak Roberts's views on race relations aren't known, but he clearly had little interest in following his father into Navarro County politics.

When Doak turned eighteen, he took a job as a grocery clerk in Corsicana but quickly left the position when signed to play for the Waco franchise of the 1888 Texas League. Naturally right-handed, an injury forced Roberts to learn to play baseball as a lefty, and he remains one of the few ambidextrous pitchers in baseball history. His professional career, however, did not last long. Just two weeks into the season, the Waco franchise folded. Roberts never received a paycheck or another contract in professional baseball. Yet he remains as one of the most important personalities in Texas League history.

By the mid-1890s, Doak Roberts set up a seed, grain and feed business in Corsicana. The many farmers of Navarro County flocked to his store, and business remained steady, receiving a boost when the railroad arrived and commercial farming increased. Though agribusiness was his livelihood, Roberts's real interest remained in baseball. If he couldn't play the game, he would make his mark as a manager and executive.

Roberts initially approached Texas League officials to place a franchise in Corsicana in the late 1890s. Oil, along with the railroad, brought great prosperity to the Navarro County seat, and Roberts felt sure he could turn the city's rapid growth into success at the ballpark. Texas League owners showed less enthusiasm. They had already committed to small-market teams in Sherman-Denison and Paris. Corsicana became just another in a long list of interested cities. Doak Roberts found himself frustrated in his efforts, and it's quite possible that by the time the eight-team Texas League folded in 1898, many owners were glad to be rid of him. But they didn't realize the persistence of Doak Roberts's character.

Navarro County residents founded Corsicana in 1848 about seventy-five miles southeast of Dallas. Originally established as the county seat, Corsicana grew slowly through the Civil War. Unlike the counties along the Red River,

By the late 1890s, oil derricks covered much of Corsicana. *Courtesy Ron Maxfield.*

Navarro County voted 99 percent in favor of secession, and local residents quickly joined the Confederate cause. Like all of Texas, Corsicana fell on hard times after the war, but fortunes changed in 1871 with the arrival of the Houston and Texas Central Railroad. When the Cotton Belt Railroad joined the HTC nine years later, Corsicana became an economic force, attracting residents, commerce and local utilities. One utility, the Corsicana Water Development Company, soon changed the city and Texas forever.

In 1894, while searching for shallow artesian water, well drillers instead struck oil, the first discovered west of the Mississippi River. Seven years before establishment of the Spindletop oil field near Beaumont, Corsicana became the oil capital of the west. Prospectors from across the United States flooded the city, erecting oil derricks on every street corner and any empty lot they might find. Residents eagerly offered their property for prospecting in return for a cut of the profits. Like Sherman and Denison, the local electrical streetcar company replaced mule-powered cars at decade's end, and Corsicana sat on the cusp of prosperity. Its conservative residents, though, abhorred the clientele attracted to the city's brothels, gambling halls and saloons.

While the Corsicana economy clung to the railroad until the oil discovery, 175 miles to the northeast, Texarkana formed from America's earliest transportation routes—Native American trails. The Great Southwest Trail,

Downtown Texarkana, circa 1905. *Author's collection.*

a centuries-old route for Indians between the Mississippi River and the West, passed directly through Texarkana, an area surrounded by Caddo settlements. By the early 1870s, railroads pushed across Arkansas toward Texas, with the Cairo and Fulton joining the Texas and Pacific a few miles west of the Red River in Arkansas. Over the next two decades, Texarkana grew in both population and stature, soon hosting a number of manufacturers such as the Texarkana Casket Company and a large cotton compress, as well as dry goods merchants, grocers and restaurants. The easternmost land route into the state became important to the economies of Northeast Texas, Southwest Arkansas and Northwest Louisiana.

By 1902, Charles W. Dewitt had opened Texarkana's Oyster Bay Restaurant with his son, Charles Jerome Dewitt, as an employee. Originally from Ohio and new to the area, the Dewitt family worked hard to establish their business and befriended a local attorney with a passion for baseball. While the younger Dewitt and the family friend shared a sporting interest, Charles had little use for the game and continued concentrating on building his restaurant business. Before long, though, the elder Dewitt found himself caught up in the same baseball fever as his son.

While 1898 through 1901 saw a dearth of professional baseball in North Texas, as 1902 approached, baseball's premier promoter returned to the state, and the Texas League once again took center stage. Both Corsicana and Texarkana soon found their brief appearances in the league among the most memorable in minor-league history.

Ted Sullivan returned to Texas fresh off a stint managing in the financially successful Southern League. Despite his previous experience in Texas, he still believed the state could support a professional league, and he expected it could do so to the financial benefit of its backers.

"My heart has been for Texas," he said. "I love her sunny skies and grassy prairies…Texas looks ripe…for not only a good baseball season in 1902 but for years to come if properly handled."

This time, Ted Sullivan brought both his support and several years more experience to the Texas League. His prediction of good baseball for years to come became prophetic.

In his years of travels and involvement in minor leagues throughout the country, Ted Sullivan learned two important things that applied to Texas baseball. First, Texans wanted to see other Texans on the diamond. Experienced minor leaguers from the east and Midwest might bring quality play to Texas, but they were not Texans. Texans demanded homegrown talent, and Sullivan knew they would fill the ballparks to see the best the state offered. Secondly, Sullivan recognized the importance of transportation, both statewide and local. Local transit systems supporting baseball supplied a steady stream of spectators, and both baseball and streetcar companies benefitted. The support of the Paris streetcar system made that city particularly attractive to Sullivan, and as 1902 approached, he made plans to field a club where E.H.R. Green had experienced some success a few years earlier.

Planners for the 1902 Texas League focused on familiar cities: Fort Worth, Houston, Sherman-Denison, Austin and Waco. Galveston lacked a stomach for baseball as it rebuilt just two years after the most destructive hurricane in U.S. history killed over six thousand of its residents. Potential newcomers Corsicana, Beaumont and El Paso all lobbied for spots in the league, seeking to benefit from Galveston's misfortune.

While South Texas franchise owners had historically been leery of their North Texas colleagues, those in the north held a mutual distrust. South Texas officials lobbied to drop various northern teams from the circuit on a seemingly annual basis, complaining of long jumps and poor gate receipts.

While North Texas baseball had been inactive since 1897, South Texas owners had continued to successfully field their own teams, and the northern owners explored starting their own league as well. After all, South Texas had proven it could survive without the northern cities. Northern owners saw no reason they could not do the same. Thus, the stage was set for several years of split professional baseball within Texas.

Ted Sullivan seemed to side with other potential North Texas owners, noting that railroads would have to offer excellent rates to make southern jumps profitable. He praised the Sherman-Denison Interurban railroad and local streetcar systems in Paris and other cities. By the end of November, owners decided to forgo the southern teams, and the seven cities of Dallas, Fort Worth, Sherman-Denison, Texarkana, Waco, Paris and Corsicana competed for spots in the six-team league. Ultimately, the sixth city came down to a choice between Texarkana and Corsicana, with reinstated president John L. Ward charged with making the final decision.

By early January 1902, Texarkana claimed to have an agreement in place to field a team with several players already under contract. With an owner for the Dallas franchise not yet secured, Ted Sullivan abandoned his plans for a team in Paris, but Charles Eisenfelder of Galveston staked his claim to the ownerless franchise. At month's end, John L. Ward chose Corsicana over Texarkana, the proximity of the city to others in the circuit and the associated travel savings the deciding factors. Corsicana's rapid growth and booming economy made it a sure bet to fill the ballpark on a daily basis.

With Corsicana selected, the Texarkana Baseball Association cried foul, declaring its elimination from contention an unwarranted and illegal breach of contract. The association claimed it had paid its league dues, and the Texas League owed it a spot on the circuit. It even offered to assist other teams with travel costs to the city, but John L. Ward was unsympathetic. He left Texarkana on the sidelines, and Corsicana prepared for its first season of professional baseball. The entire baseball world would soon take notice.

The Corsicana Baseball Association, having secured its spot in the Texas League with a $2,500 franchise fee, rapidly fueled local fan enthusiasm. The association named Corsicana Cotton Compress manager Upton Blair general manager, Doak Roberts secretary and A.L Blassingame field manager. Local fans staked a spot to hang what they believed the inevitable pennant in Corsicana's ballpark, a diamond within a ten-minute walk of anywhere in the city, now the intersection of Ninth and Tenth Streets. In February, many arrangements already in place, Blair and Roberts showed off the team's gray-and-black uniforms with "Oil Citys" emblazoned across

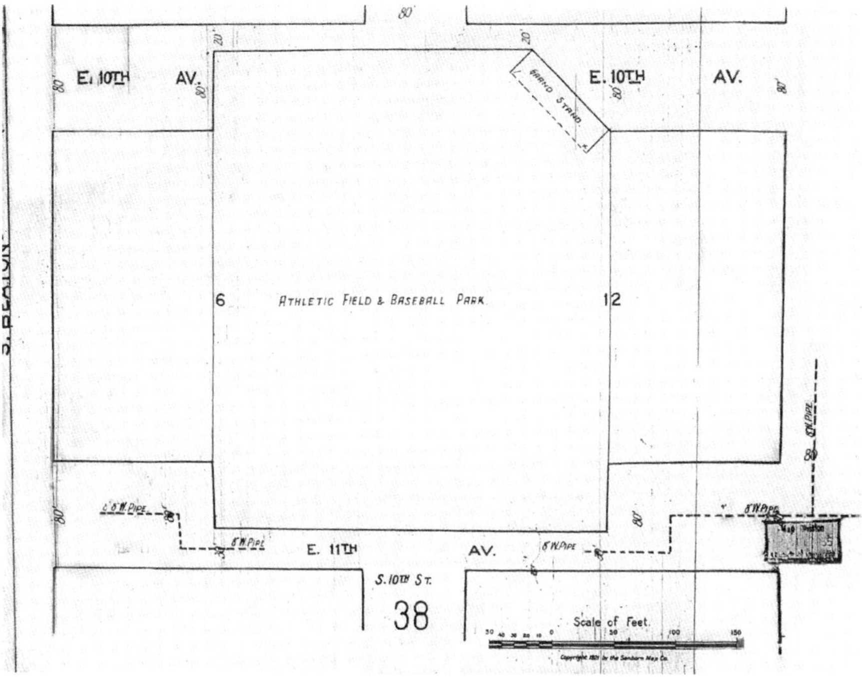

Layout of the Corsicana 1902 ball field, home of the Texas League champion Corsicana Oil Citys. *Courtesy Ron Maxfield.*

the chest. Their most important personnel move involved signing Big Mike O'Connor as manager, his ability to get the best out of even amateur players making him a natural selection. By late March, under the guidance of Doak Roberts and Mike O'Connor, Upton Blair signed a number of players who, together, would become legendary in minor-league baseball. Infielders Bill Alexander, Walter Morris and George Markley joined first baseman O'Connor, and Jay "Nig" Clarke assumed catching duties. The pitching staff included William "Lucky" Wright, Bellmont Method and Robert White, and the outfield Ike Pendleton, Frank Ripley and thirteen-year veteran James "Curley" Maloney. With longtime Texas Leaguer Ben Shelton later joining the club, Corsicana's management assembled a formidable franchise, and the rest of the Texas League took note.

While Corsicana looked forward to its first season in the Texas League, farther north along the Houston and Texas Central, Cy Mulkey arranged another joint Sherman-Denison franchise. J.P. Crearer convinced Mulkey that his Woodlake Park, midway between the two cities, would be a logical

Cy Mulkey (upper left), a Texas League player, manager and umpire, also coached the Austin College baseball team in 1907. *Author's collection.*

home for the franchise, equally accessible to fans from both north and south. The centrally located ballpark would discourage the jealousy that doomed previous joint franchises in the cities, and it ensured Crearer a profit from Interurban passengers. Mulkey thought Crearer's business plan a good one. It wasn't long before he realized the error of his agreement.

Alvin Lee "Cy" Mulkey once reigned as one of the Texas League's best-known players. Merely an adequate fielder, a below-average hitter and only a stopgap pitcher, Mulkey focused on strategy as a well-known student of the game. He played on enough Texas League franchises to experience the best and worst of league operations, and his experience in the cotton business and civic affairs made him an ideal team owner.

Born in Tom Bean, close to Kentuckytown in Grayson County, Cy Mulkey grew up on a farm and pursued a variety of interests, including agriculture, law and a stint as justice of the peace. During the 1890s, he retired from baseball on more than one occasion, but the allure of the game continued to bring him back. Likely Grayson County's most well-known baseball personality, Mulkey had two daughters who influenced his acceptance of the Sherman-Denison franchise, as they would soon be attending college in Sherman. Despite his travels, Mulkey never lost his affinity for Grayson County, even returning to Sherman to coach the Austin College ball club later in the decade and building a house at the end of Robertson Street in Tom Bean. In 1902, though, Cy Mulkey concentrated his attention on another Sherman-Denison entrant in the Texas League. Not to be outdone by his old friend Mike O'Connor in Corsicana, even before he secured a ballpark, Mulkey showed off the Sherman-Denison Blues' new uniforms—navy blue with cardinal trim and Norfolk jackets, surely to be the most stylish in the league.

While Cy Mulkey may have outdone Mike O'Connor in appearance, he fell short in assembling talent. An infield consisting of Mulkey, Dred Cavender, Roland Wolfe and Red Welter backed pitching ace Howard Murphy. Sam Deskin, Don Curtis and Tom Gillon made up the outfield, while A.L. Blassingame, released as manager of Corsicana after the arrival of Mike O'Connor, filled out the roster as catcher.

No one questioned Cy Mulkey's heart when it came to baseball or his interest in making Sherman-Denison a successful stop on the Texas League circuit. In Charles Eisenfelder, though, Paris had an unknown commodity with unknown aspirations. In fact, Eisenfelder himself had little idea of his aspirations. He seemed to be searching for his niche—a niche eluding him for several years. The son of German immigrants, Eisenfelder arrived in the United States as a five year-old in 1868, settling in Galveston shortly after the yellow fever epidemic of the early 1870s. By the time the Eisenfelder family arrived, Galveston boasted the largest population of any Texas community, and its port made it arguably the state's most important city. By the late 1800s, Galveston offered almost limitless opportunities for an enterprising man, and Eisenfelder savvied himself as just that.

Throughout the 1890s, Eisenfelder dabbled as a book dealer, wholesaler, clerk and collector but found little satisfaction in any of the fields. His erratic personality often surfaced, and Eisenfelder regularly feuded with those he felt slighted him, suing city officials over the local fire brigade's response to an emergency at his seed warehouse and what he deemed unreasonable business taxes. Despite his difficult nature, though, Eisenfelder remained involved in civic affairs and social circles.

One of Eisenfelder's many hats included that of Galveston's boxing commissioner. While his success or failure in the position is not recorded, the sporting bug apparently sat well with him. Eisenfelder became involved with Galveston's professional baseball franchise of 1899, and after both he and his Galveston home survived the 1900 hurricane relatively unscathed, Eisenfelder actively pursued a future in baseball management.

When Charles Eisenfelder learned of Ted Sullivan's intention to abandon Paris for Dallas, he quickly traveled to Lamar County and joined forces with the new streetcar company. Eisenfelder secured his team with a $250 performance guarantee and soon found himself appointed to the league's scheduling committee. Ironically, his most memorable mark on Texas League history eventually resulted from his indifference to the schedule he helped create.

His franchise in place, Eisenfelder returned to Galveston to arrange his affairs, soon arriving back in Paris on E.H.R. Green's Texas Midland Railroad. He arranged for a new ballpark on the edge of the city, convinced the Paris Traction Company to expand streetcar service in its direction and ordered smart-looking silver-gray uniforms with maroon trim along with a rail car full of baseball equipment. He hinted at a preference for classy players, boasting to have reviewed eight hundred applicants and signing only those with the highest personal and professional standards.

Known informally as the Parisians, Paris's 1902 franchise featured three managers over the course of the season: Emmett Rogers of Arkansas, native New Yorker and Texas League Hall of Famer Wilson Matthews and former championship-winning manager Wade Moore. Aside from Moore at catcher and Rogers at first base, Eisenfelder filled the Paris roster with utility players, forcing his managers to juggle the lineup on a seemingly daily basis. Tom Dugan, Roy Akin, Bert Adrian and Ed Pleiss all saw extended action in the field, while Carl "Bones" France, a place-hitting outfielder, brought his slender frame and bat to town as well.

Local product Tony Thebo, the quick-footed son who George Thebo had taken to semipro ballgames a few years earlier, joined the Parisians in the outfield. Having returned to Paris in 1900 after attending a private academy in his mother's hometown of St. Louis, Thebo played center field and gained a reputation as a prolific base stealer. He also developed a right arm capable of throwing out a base runner from center field virtually flat-footed. For Thebo, his return to Paris was bittersweet. George Thebo, who longed to see Tony in professional baseball, passed away after suffering a stroke a year earlier. Based on league records, he never saw Tony play a game. Yet an unpublished Thebo family history reveals he may actually have had the opportunity before his death:

Tony's heart stayed in baseball. A terrific family excitement came on when Tony stated, one spring vacation, that he was going to play professional ball that summer.

"Never!" Gran (Mary Thebo) snorted, making an end of the matter.

"I've signed a contract to play," Tony said.

"A son of mine on the professional baseball diamond? Never!"

"I've already signed up," Tony repeated patiently.

"Thebo on a baseball contract?" Gran roared. "Never!"

"It's already there," Tony said.

"It will come off!" The rafters began to shake. "Debase your name—my name—in such a way! It will come off whatever you signed! Do you hear me, Sir? It will come off!"

It did. But Tony played that summer just the same—under an assumed name. Perhaps George Thebo did the same as a spectator.

As Cy Mulkey and Charles Eisenfelder worked to assemble competitive franchises, even league stalwarts William H. Ward and Joe Gardner could concoct nothing to compete with Corsicana's Doak Roberts. The Oil Citys ran away with the 1902 season from the start. Mike O'Connor, an off-season railroad worker and "one of the hardest hitters ever," led his team on an early season tear as Corsicana won eleven of its first thirteen games. Pitchers held O'Connor in terror, and the speed of the Oil Citys slowed only when they "feared they would be charley-horsed from over-exertion." Like Corsicana, Paris also started the season quickly, winning seven of its first nine. Pitcher Rick Adams's rhythm on the mound set the stage for a potent offense averaging nine runs a game in the season's first week.

Fast starts from Corsicana and Paris spelled misery for Sherman-Denison and Grayson County baseball kranks. Dropping five of six to the Parisians to start the season, the Tigers followed with six straight losses at home to Corsicana and Waco. Dismal attendance only added to the frustration. Cy Mulkey's allegiances may have been in Grayson County but not at the expense of successful baseball, and certainly not at the expense of his financial investment. He soon realized the tactical error of his agreement to play in Woodlake Park. While J.P. Crearer and other backers expected Woodlake to be a convenient site for baseball fans of both cities, it was, in fact, inconvenient to all. Baseball fans might be willing to walk a few blocks to the ballpark or even invest a nickel in streetcar fare, but a twenty-five-cent round trip to Woodlake Park was both time-consuming and expensive. The added expense of a ticket to the baseball game placed the cost of a trip to the ballpark beyond the budget of many fans. The businessman in Cy Mulkey knew that the existence of his franchise required a radical decision. Disgusted with support both on and off the field, on May 8, Mulkey announced he was moving his franchise to Texarkana, the same city that had denounced the Texas League's integrity a few months earlier. Unfortunately for both Texarkana and Cy Mulkey, scenery did not change the club's fortunes.

Paris native and career minor leaguer Tony Thebo. *Author's collection.*

The Texarkana Casketmakers, as they became known, claimed a ballpark east of the railroad tracks and southeast of the casket factory, beneath what is now the West Eighth Street overpass. Over the next month, the Casketmakers suffered numerous lopsided losses, held to fewer than three runs on eighteen occasions and shut out five times. By the time it limped into Corsicana for a three-game series in mid-June, Texarkana found itself buried in last place. Corsicana, riding a six-game winning streak and coming off a series in which it outscored Paris by a soon-to-be ironic score of 51–3, rode high atop the league, led by a hard-hitting offense and some of the most outstanding pitching Texas League fans ever witnessed.

The Casketmakers dropped the first two games in Corsicana, but the 6–5 and 9–2 losses weren't nearly as embarrassing as some of their recent games. First baseman Jerome Dewitt joined the team when it arrived in Texarkana and proved to be the only spark of an inept offense, eventually batting .340 for the season. As the Casketmakers warmed up for the final game of the Corsicana series on June 15, though, Dewitt did not realize that he was about to make professional baseball history.

Even in the early twentieth century, several sizable Texas cities—including Corsicana—continued to outlaw Sunday baseball. Nearby Waco passed ordinances against Sunday games as well, and though rumors of the state legislature taking action spread across Texas, as of June 1902, organized Sunday baseball remained illegal. With his ballpark effectively closed down for the June 15 game and Waco not an option, Doak Roberts arranged for the finale of the Texarkana series to be played on a makeshift field a few miles north in Ennis. Local historians report that the game was played in a small ballpark at the corner of South McKinney and Crockett Streets, about three blocks southwest of the depot. Assuming the streets have not been adjusted since 1902, a look at a modern map or aerial photo reveals the block to be rather small to host a professional baseball game, leading credence to the claims of many that the Ennis field was far smaller than a standard ballpark. In fact, some claimed the right field fence to be only about forty feet beyond first base, and depending on the original layout of the ballpark, the claim is indeed possible. Legends have clouded the facts, though, and others described the field as perfectly adequate for professional baseball. Regardless, there is no doubt that tiny Ennis, Texas, became the unlikely site of what was to become one of baseball's most memorable afternoons.

When Jerome Dewitt began to excel at first base, his father, Charles, redirected his interest from the restaurant business to baseball. In fact, he approached Cy Mulkey about becoming involved with the team on a financial basis, and Mulkey, with no deep pockets of his own and in need of local support, quickly took Dewitt up on his offer. The elder Dewitt's involvement, though, apparently gave young Jerome a sense of entitlement. Arriving late at the Ennis ballpark, Jerome informed Mulkey that his father wanted him to pitch, a position he had yet to play and certainly not against a team as potent as the Oil Citys. Though Mulkey's affinity for cursing undoubtedly came into great use at the intrusion on his managing the ball club, he obliged Dewitt, who promptly took the mound.

The composition of the official box score of the game has been disputed since Corsicana recorded the final out, but no one questioned the outcome of the June 15, 1902 contest. Corsicana battered Jerome Dewitt all afternoon, pounding out an obscene fifty-three hits in a 51–3 shellacking, the most lopsided score in any professional baseball game before or since. Catcher Nig Clarke led the Oil City attack, smashing eight home runs, another professional baseball record. While some claimed Clarke's home runs as nothing more than pop-ups over a short right field fence, years later,

Downtown Ennis, Texas, circa 1905. *Courtesy Ennis Chamber of Commerce.*

Jay "Nig" Clarke hit eight home runs in Corsicana's 51–3 victory over Texarkana in 1902. *Author's collection.*

BOX SCORE: CORSICANA VS. TEXARKANA AT ENNIS, JUNE 15, 1902

Corsicana	AB	R	H	Texarkana	AB	R	H
Maloney, cf	6	5	3	Deskin, cf	5	1	2
Alexander, 2b	8	5	8	Mulkey, 2b	4	0	1
Ripley, rf	8	6	5	Welter, 3b	4	0	1
Pendleton, lf	8	6	8	Wolfe, c	4	1	1
Markley, 3b	7	7	6	Murphey, lf	4	0	1
O'Connor, 1b	8	7	7	DeWitt, p	3	0	1
Clark, c	8	8	8	Tackaberry, 1b	4	1	1
Morris, ss	8	6	6	Gillon, rf	4	0	1
Wright, p	4	1	2	Burns, ss	4	0	0
	65	51	53		36	3	9

Stolen Bases: *Maloney, Alexander, Morris, Clark, Ripley.* **Home Runs:** *Clark (8), O'Connor (3), Alexander (3), Ripley (2), Pendleton (2), Maloney, Markley, Morris.* **Triples:** *Markley, O'Connor.* **Doubles:** *Morris, Alexander, Maloney, Pendleton, Deskin, Tackaberry, Welter.* **LOB:** *Corsicana (15), Texarkana (5).* **Errors:** *Corsicana (0), Texarkana (5).* **Double Plays By:** *Corsicana (4), Texarkana (1).* **Walks By:** *Wright (1), DeWitt (3).* **Struck Out By:** *Wright (2), DeWitt (1).* **Hit By Pitcher By:** *DeWitt (3).* **Earned Runs By:** *Corsicana (26), Texarkana (1).* **Umpires:** *Method and Cavender.* **Time:** *2:10.*

Texarkana	*010*	*000*	*020—3*
Corsicana	*629*	*275*	*488—51*

Unofficial box score of Corsicana's June 15, 1902 victory over the Texarkana Casketmakers. *Courtesy Ron Maxfield.*

he recounted the game and insisted his record completely legitimate. Bill Alexander and Mike O'Connor added three home runs apiece, as Corsicana slammed a total of twenty-one homers on the day to go along with seven doubles and two triples.

Cy Mulkey's refusal to remove Dewitt from the game became legendary. With the score 17–1 after three innings, bench players began to call for Dewitt's relief, but Mulkey simply leaned against a post and chewed harder on his tobacco. Three innings later, with the score 31–1, they again asked Mulkey when he would put poor Jerome out of his misery. Mulkey responded famously and unapologetically, "His daddy said he's going to pitch, and he's sure pitching, ain't he?"

Indeed, Jerome Dewitt did pitch, and by day's end, he went down in professional baseball lore as having put on what remains the worst performance in baseball history. A few games later, Dewitt resurfaced briefly on the mound, allowing just one hit in two innings of work. Still, his fifty-one runs, fifty-four hits and twenty-one home runs surrendered in eleven innings are marks of futility that have remained unsurpassed for over a century. Dewitt could take some solace in his performance, though; after all, opponents earned only twenty-six of the fifty-one runs he allowed.

Following the embarrassment in Corsicana, Mulkey was not long for Texarkana. Just a few days after returning to the city, he left the team in C.B. Dewitt's hands and returned to Grayson County, stating that he was retiring from baseball for good. Ted Sullivan talked him into yet another comeback, though, and just a few days later, Mulkey found himself on the Dallas Giants diamond. C.B. Dewitt, on the other hand, had less staying power. By July 8, the Texarkana Casketmakers, not Cy Mulkey, found themselves out of the league, disbanding with a 21-46 record. Soon, the Dewitt family left Texarkana, relocating to Mineral Wells, where young Jerome underwent unsuccessful treatment for tuberculosis. Less than two years after his historic performance in Corsicana, Jerome Dewitt died at the age of twenty-two. For several years, his parents operated the Hotel Jerome in Mineral Wells before opening a therapeutic well themselves and dabbling in other tourist attractions. After 1902, C.B. Dewitt's name is not recorded in organized baseball records again, and Texarkana failed in its one shot to field a Texas League franchise.

As the 1902 season moved into summer, Corsicana's domination of the Texas League grew legendary. Paris experienced financial difficulties to the point that Charles Eisenfelder announced he would relocate his team to Houston as attendance in Paris was not profitable. Other owners objected, however, and Eisenfelder countered by refusing to play scheduled home games for most of the remainder of the season, willing to accept the visitor's fifty-dollar guarantee over losing money in Paris. In the midst of a twenty-seven-game road trip, the Parisians found themselves unofficially rebranded as "Eisenfelder's Homeseekers," a name following the team throughout Texas League history. The toll of the road far too much to bear, the Paris season that had begun so promisingly in Sherman-Denison ended with the team forty and a half games out of first place with a 44-61 record. The few bright spots included Tony Thebo's .310 batting average and thirty-eight stolen bases, along with pitcher Rick Adams's eighteen wins and .330 batting average.

While Paris struggled to string together more than a victory or two, between June 8 and July 5, the Corsicana Oil Citys posted a record twenty-seven-game winning streak. Finally broken in a 3–1 loss to Waco behind the pitching of "Dad" Ahorn, over the course of the streak, Corsicana's Lucky Wright won ten games, including both ends of a double-header on June

Left: George "Lucky" Wright, a member of several champion clubs over the course of his career. *Author's collection.*

Below: The 1902 Texas League champion Corsicana Oil Citys are regarded by many as among the best professional baseball clubs ever assembled. *Author's collection.*

29. The potent lineup outscored its opponents 287–80 during the streak, and the resulting .864 winning percentage (57-9) in the season's first half under Mike O'Connor remains a Texas League record. Though slipping to a second-half record of 30-14, Corsicana's overall 87-23 mark left them twenty-eight and a half games ahead of second-place Dallas at season's end. Lucky Wright led the pitching staff with thirty-five wins, followed by Belmont Method and Robert White with twenty-eight and twenty, respectively. Although managers relied on relief pitchers only rarely during the Deadball Era, the endurance of Corsicana's pitching staff remains unsurpassed. No reliever appeared the entire season, every outing recorded as a complete game for the starting pitcher. Corsicana led the league in virtually all hitting categories, including a .276 team average, 256 extra base hits and forty-six home runs, an extremely large number for the Deadball Era. Impressively, Oil Citys base runners stole 244 bases, with six players registering over 25 each. Lucky Wright's thirty-five wins, forty-two complete games and 385 innings pitched remain Texas League records over a century later. Their team's winning percentage and statistics notched in the record books, in early September, Oil Citys fans made plans to raise the pennant on the pole erected just for that purpose months earlier.

While some expected Corsicana's 1902 dominance to negatively impact Texas baseball, it contrarily placed the Texas League on the national stage. Never before had a team so dominated a circuit, and the 51–3 victory over Texarkana made sports headlines nationwide. Aside from the failure of Cy Mulkey's franchise and Charles Eisenfelder's ongoing disputes with league owners, the 1902 season was a rousing success. Ted Sullivan's decade-old prediction of Texas as a baseball profit base began to take shape.

CHAPTER 10

1903: COMPETITIVE BALANCE

Preparations for the 1903 season began immediately after Corsicana took the 1902 pennant. For the first time in several years, owners statewide seriously considered the consolidation of North and South Texas teams. Early favorites included Fort Worth, Dallas, Corsicana, Beaumont and Houston, with New Orleans and Shreveport as out-of-state contenders. Franchise owners agreed that such a league made sense both geographically and financially. It only took until early September before Ted Sullivan began to get new ideas.

Ever the strategist, Sullivan still favored North Texas teams and proposed a league including ten teams, with San Antonio, Austin, Galveston and Waco added to the mix and the Louisiana teams dropped. While some North Texas owners remained leery of working with their counterparts in the south, Sullivan believed statewide competition remained a key to eventual success and that the continued operation of two leagues would result in neither prospering. As far as Sullivan was concerned, Dallas, Fort Worth, Corsicana and Paris had proven their worth and could remain on the circuit as long as they received support. He proposed adding four South Texas teams to be chosen from six cities and remained open to adding two additional cities if suitors could be found.

By November, league officials assured Dallas, Fort Worth, Corsicana, Houston and San Antonio spots on the circuit, with Paris expected to return upon Ted Sullivan's approval. Likewise, he considered franchises in Oklahoma City and Guthrie, but neither panned out. In fact, all earlier plans for a statewide Texas League fell apart by the end of the year, and North Texas owners decided to return with another four-team format (Corsicana, Dallas, Fort Worth and Paris) and a split season planned from the start. Although a supporter of Waco in place of Paris, Ted Sullivan took control of the Paris franchise and named it the Steers, but "Parisites" or "Parasites" remained the most widely used moniker among the media. Signing proven talent in Cy Mulkey, Roland Wolfe and Mickey Coyle, Sullivan purchased the services of former Fort Worth Panthers Reeve McKay and Clyde Bateman for his pitching staff.

South Texas owners countered Ted Sullivan's organization with their own league, offering higher salaries than North Texas owners, with Beaumont especially spending freely. Stars like Dad Ahorn, Roy Akin, Walter Morris and Lucky Wright all bolted south either before or early in the season, leaving North Texas teams to fill out their rosters with less expensive alternatives. For northern teams, the opportunity gave rise to new stars like Charley Moran, Art Morgan, Bert Hise, Reeve McKay and Clyde Bateman. Corsicana's field players remained largely intact to start the season with one notable exception. Catcher, slugger and record-breaker Nig Clarke had left the Oil Citys for Little Rock of the Southern Association, sold for a sum of fifty dollars. Likewise, little of Corsicana's record-breaking pitching staff returned, but Doak Roberts held high hopes for a second consecutive championship in the Oil City.

Before the 1903 season began, North Texas League owners faced sorrow and instability. League president John L. Ward, who had been battling kidney disease for several months, died in Fort Worth on February 21. Ward's legacy to the Texas League, however brief, included serving as an impartial force on the league's return in the mid-1890s, saving the league from collapse when Sherman abruptly ceased operations in 1896 and returning to serve an additional term in 1902 following a nearly four-year hiatus of baseball in North Texas. Owners honored Ward at their March meeting, resolving to place a wreath on his Fort Worth grave. Likewise, they elected Newton Lassiter of Fort Worth as president and H.J. McCade of Paris as second in command. Lassiter, a lawyer and insurance official, brought a wealth of experience to the league, having been involved in civic affairs, including terms as alderman, water commissioner and a railroad lawyer. Furthermore, he had experience in public recreation, serving a stint on the Lake Worth Commission. By late April, the league schedule was set. Play would begin in Corsicana on April 28, with a parade, a speech from the mayor and the official raising of the 1902 pennant.

Despite Corsicana's 1902 dominance and the return of manager Mike O'Connor, Bill Alexander, James Maloney, Ben Shelton and Hunter Hill,

Ted Sullivan's Paris Steers set the tone for 1903 from the outset. Winners of fifteen of their first twenty-one games and led by pitchers Clyde Bateman and Reeve McKay, the Steers defeated Corsicana in five consecutive games in mid-May, the first time the Oil Citys franchise had ever lost more than three games in a row. The most memorable of the wins took place on May 14, when Paris hitters battered Oil Citys pitching for nine home runs en route to a 13–7 win. Paris hurler Clyde Bateman earned the win and bested Roland Wolfe's three homers by batting five for five with four home runs and a triple. Though not as lopsided as Corsicana's win over Texarkana a year earlier, the remaining Oil Citys players must have felt a sense of payback as Paris continued to knock pitches over the fence. Later in the month, Paris took four of five from Dallas, scoring sixty-six runs in the series. The team developed a knack for late inning comebacks and a never-say-die attitude that should have been popular with local spectators. As May drew to a close, the Steers sat comfortably in first place, four games ahead of Corsicana. Parisians had never seen such quality baseball.

Ted Sullivan's true intentions for locating his team in Paris will never be known, but he developed a reputation as an elitist who expected locals to feel indebted to him for bringing his franchise to their city. Unsuccessfully attempting to coerce local reporters into writing only positive articles on his franchise, he squabbled with newspapermen incessantly, actually revoking former Paris team secretary Sandy Neville's press credentials. As fan enthusiasm began to dry up, Sullivan attempted to make amends, but reporters did not oblige. Sullivan had convinced Neville and others his interests lay only in personal financial gain and refused to offer free publicity.

Despite the Steers' on-field success, local baseball "fans" (a term Ted Sullivan personally coined to describe baseball spectators) did not turn out in numbers to meet Sullivan's expectations. On June 6, Doak Roberts and Ted Sullivan met secretly with intentions of relocating a June 14 game to Sullivan's original choice of cities, Waco. The game turned out to be wildly successful at the gate, drawing 1,200 spectators. With pressure on the team to relocate increasing, Paris played out its road trip and finished the first half of the season with a city-best 32-20 record, a full eight games ahead of second-place Dallas. Regardless of its on-field success, quietly and with little resistance, Sullivan relocated his team to Waco for the season's second half, satisfying both himself and other owners who despised the jump from the Dallas–Fort Worth area to Lamar County.

While Sullivan took a successful franchise to Waco, its neighbor to the northeast never regained its 1902 success. Corsicana manager Mike

Longtime Texas Leaguers Hunter Hill and Ben Shelton. *Courtesy Ron Maxfield.*

O'Connor played in only fifty-five games, batting a career-low .188 with only seven extra-base hits. While Ben Shelton and James Maloney continued their steady play, and newly acquired Tony Thebo stole twenty-one bases, the pitching staff showed little of its dazzling 1902 performance. Bert Hise managed a 20-10 record, but second-string pitcher Earl Zook lost a league-leading twenty-one games. At least eleven other pitchers attempted to fill the gaps during the season, but Corsicana's 23-29 first-half record left it in last place. While the Oil Citys played better in the second half, they never gained consistency, and if not for winning eight of nine games to close the season, they would have finished far worse than their 31-25 record. Regardless, its 54-54 overall mark left the team seven games out of first place.

While Corsicana faltered, Ted Sullivan's relocated Waco Steers couldn't take advantage. On-field success in Paris may not have bred local enthusiasm, but enthusiasm in Waco did not breed victories. The Steers went into a second-half swoon, finishing in last place with a 20-36 record, sixteen games behind first-place Dallas, its only real highlight being Clyde Bateman's no-hitter against Fort Worth on July 11.

Although Dallas clearly outclassed the Steers, league rules called for a championship series between the first- and second-half champions. With all games played in Dallas in front of large crowds, Waco put up little contest. Dallas took the league championship seven games to three. Ted Sullivan's move to Waco had backfired, and he must have feared that his reputation as a baseball man had taken an equal hit.

The half season of 1903 represented Paris's most successful baseball season to date. While fans may have been happy with Ted Sullivan's departure, they

CORSICANA BASEBALL TEAM.
Champions of Texas League, Season of 1904.

The 1903 Corsicana Texas League franchise could not match the success of its 1902 predecessor. *Author's collection.*

were disappointed in knowing they would almost assuredly not maintain the services of power pitcher Reeve McKay with his seventeen victories and .272 batting average. Likewise, they soon learned that Clyde Bateman, who topped McKay's success with eighteen wins, would take his arm, .344 batting average and thirteen home runs to Milwaukee of the American Association. While Paris rooters looked forward to re-obtaining a franchise in 1904, they feared they might never see the likes of McKay and Bateman in a home uniform again. Over a century later, with any Parisian who had seen the 1903 Steers in action long deceased, Paris's most successful Texas League season regained the spotlight, if only briefly, as Clyde Bateman was elected to the Texas League Hall of Fame.

CHAPTER 11

1904: SMALL CITIES SANDWICH THE LEAGUE

Planning for the 1904 season began in early October with owners considering a southwestern league including the 1903 North Texas teams as well as Oklahoma City and Shawnee, Oklahoma. Meanwhile, some favored an alternate plan of dropping the Oklahoma teams and adding Houston, Galveston and Beaumont. Owners remained adamant, however, that good baseball cities be selected. After years of juggling franchises, they wanted stability. Likewise, the public wanted to see the best talent available. Franchises in cities that couldn't support increased salaries need not apply.

In early 1904, new league president William Alexander "Alex" Abbey accepted applications for a fourth North Texas franchise from Sherman, Paris and Ardmore and McAlester in Oklahoma. Abbey, a Fort Worth newspaperman, came to Texas from Maryland in 1870. A civil engineer by trade, Abbey had served as W.H. Ward's scorekeeper for several seasons before launching the *Fort Worth Evening News*.

Early on, Ardmore appeared to be William Abbey's leading candidate for a new franchise, while Ted Sullivan lobbied to move his franchise from Waco to Denison. When suitable grounds couldn't be secured in Ardmore, however, Paris became the next logical choice. It had a reputation for at least moderate success at the gate and, in the right situation, had proven it could support a team. In the end, despite all the jockeying for position, the North Texas League began the season with the same four cities it had begun with a year earlier.

E.H.R. Green, with his virtually limitless resources, and Ted Sullivan, a baseball magnate, were the type of individuals one would expect to own a baseball team. But ownership of a minor-league franchise in the early years of professional baseball was not merely for the wealthy or well connected. The ability to secure a franchise relied as much as anything on an owner's contacts in a city where the league had an interest. Few owners of the time had the finances to construct a stadium, equip a team and pay salaries and travel expenses. Yet even in today's dollars, franchise fees were negligible. The $2,500 Paris offered to put up in 1897 was an enormously large sum for the time, with Eisenfelder's 1902 $250 guarantee more typical. Local stock companies often backed teams and operated on small investments from a number of individuals rather than an independent owner. With infighting among owners in stock arrangements common, most leagues preferred to avoid the notoriously unstable franchises.

Following the 1903 season, Paris baseball supporters proposed a stock arrangement allowing the city to field a Texas League club the following year. Dallas manager J.W. Gardner, a vocal critic of stock-supported teams, publicly stated his opposition to Paris's proposal. As late as Thanksgiving, city officials still lobbied for a spot on the circuit, but the influential Gardner refused to budge from his position. Soon, Paris officials redirected their attention to an Interstate League with teams in Paris and Texarkana, Texas; Fort Smith and Searcy, Arkansas; and Durant and Ardmore, Oklahoma. Despite the efforts of organizers in all cities, however, the league never came to fruition. In January 1904, the Paris baseball community watched the Texas League admit franchises in Dallas, Fort Worth and Corsicana, with the fourth awarded to Fort Worth residents William Miller and Guy Rall. As Miller and Rall had already expressed interest in placing their team in Ardmore, Oklahoma, it appeared Paris, a four-year member of the Texas League, would be left out.

Blue-collar men did not usually own baseball teams. Even in the early twentieth century, a baseball operation required a substantial investment, and without a well-financed independent owner or stock arrangement, no team could remain viable. William Miller, a twenty-five-year-old Kentucky native, was a "newspaper man" according to the *Dallas Morning News*, a position highly respected at the time. In reality, however, Miller labored as a typesetter with little experience in the business world, much less in operating a baseball team. His partner Guy Rall, one of seven children and a descendant of Texas pioneer and Indian fighter Amos Rall [Rawls], operated as a "big furniture dealer" in Fort Worth. As with Miller, the report was an exaggeration. In reality, Rall, at the time only twenty-three years old, was a macaroni salesman, but he did enter the furniture business later in life.

Perhaps Miller, as a typesetter, had connections to Texas League president and newspaper owner William Abbey. Regardless, neither he nor his partner had any experience managing a baseball club.

Despite attempts to locate their franchise in Ardmore, Miller and Rall could not come to an agreement with the city officials who, like Paris, watched their city benefit from a new relationship with the Santa Fe Railroad. The season rapidly approaching and their investment in danger of collapse, the co-owners of the homeless franchise searched for another host city. Paris, with its two-year-old ballpark ready for immediate play, became the obvious choice. Texas League officials familiar with other owners' concerns about traveling eastward from Dallas offered little enthusiasm for the choice. With time short, however, failure to quickly designate a fourth city meant the season would be lost. League officials reluctantly accepted Paris as its fourth franchise for 1904. Perhaps in honor of Paris's taking advantage of Ardmore's misfortune, the media dubbed the team the Parasites. Officially, though, Miller and Rall named their team the Red Ravens.

Paris's 1904 roster bore little resemblance to those of the previous two years. Successful pitchers Rick Adams, Reeve McKay and Clyde Bateman had all moved on, and Paris youngster Tony Thebo had found a home elsewhere in Texas. Miller and Rall did successfully lure 1902 Corsicana manager Mike O'Connor to lead the team, but he had little luck assembling a competitive roster. Field players Sam Deskin, Clark Spencer and Pete Walsh hit lightly on their best days. The pitching staff, anchored by second-year players Earl Zook, Al Selby and August Hamilton, combined for only a 29-31 record. O'Connor worried that his team may not even be competitive, and for good reason.

Disappointed in his team's 1903 performance, Corsicana owner Doak Roberts retooled his team in the off-season. Manager James Maloney led the team, with Walter Salm, Frank Coyle, Harry Longley and Tony Thebo headlining the lineup. Newcomer Tom "the Snake Charmer" Huddleston anchored the pitching staff, backed by Belmont Method and Bert Hise, holdovers from the 1902 championship team.

The renamed Corsicana Oilers started the 1904 season strongly, winning seventeen of their first twenty-two games. Huddleston led outstanding Oiler pitching, allowing no more than three runs in thirteen of their early season games, including four shutouts. Despite the team's success, though, patronage disappointed Doak Roberts. His threat to move the team to untested Oklahoma City spurned local citizens to attempt to purchase the team, but the disorganized group could not raise sufficient funds. With the first-place Oilers in danger of leaving town, 1902 team organizer Upton Blair stepped in and bought out Doak Roberts. Five days later, Corsicana finished the first half in familiar territory—atop the Texas League with a 32-20 record.

Perhaps Doak Roberts knew patronage was not the Oilers' only problem when he sold his franchise. Before the second half began, team leaders Tony Thebo and Harry Longley bolted for higher salaries in South Texas. After four consecutive wins, Corsicana fell on hard times, playing .500 ball until mid-July before finishing the season losing seventeen of its last twenty-one games. Curley Maloney resigned as manager, leaving the team in the hands of an equally unsuccessful Walter Salm for the season's last two weeks. The Oilers closed the season with just two wins in their last thirteen games.

While Corsicana fell apart on the field, former team owner Doak Roberts worked to entrench himself as a league executive. When William Abbey abruptly resigned as Texas League president on July 13, team owners elected Roberts to fill his slot. He would go on to serve as president for thirteen of the next twenty-five seasons, sporadically dabbling in the league as an owner.

While Corsicana's fortunes literally and figuratively traveled south in the season's second half, Paris didn't stand a chance from opening day. The Parasites' 1904 season began in Dallas on April 27, where Paris took two of three games. The brief success encouraged Miller and Rall, but the subsequent trip to Fort Worth brought them back to reality as they watched their team lose three consecutive games, including 18–0 and 5–0 shutouts, the latter with William Abbey in attendance. The team's return to a rain-soaked home diamond on Pine Bluff Street in Paris proved little advantage, as it dropped five of its first seven home games, including two extra-inning losses to Fort Worth. Paris did gain an extra home game when Corsicana agreed to relocate their May 9 game to the city to take advantage of crowds expected for Paris's street fair. The Parasites seized the opportunity and squeezed out a 3–2 win. Regardless, after the game, the team boarded a train for Corsicana with just a 4-9 record.

Miller and Rall watched grimly as their team finished May with fourteen more losses and a five-game losing streak marked by an inability to hit, field or prevent the opposing team from scoring. On June 1, the Parasites found themselves in last place with a 9-23 record, already fourteen games behind Corsicana. Paris fans did take pride in a 7–0 loss to Corsicana on May 26, however, as local boys Tony Thebo, Frank Coyle and Ben Shelton played well for the Oil City team, and Paris First National Bank teller Jack Bankhead pitched the shutout. With no ties to Paris, William Miller failed to join in on the local pride and bailed on his team and business partner, returning to Fort Worth and his job with the newspaper.

Early June brought unusually heavy rains to northeast Texas, with some areas receiving up to ten inches during the month. Rain washed out six Paris games in the month's first three weeks, but the most devastating blow occurred when a major rail line between Paris and Dallas washed out in Hunt County. With travel difficult, Guy Rall moved all games on the road. The Parasites played twenty-seven straight away from home, managing victories in only three games. With losing streaks of eleven and ten games, the team averaged only two runs in each of its twenty-four losses, including three games played on June 12–13 in which it managed to score a total of just one run. Exhausted, the Parasites finally returned home after Independence Day to rumors that they would soon be transferred to Ardmore. Remaining in Paris only long enough to lose four straight games to Fort Worth, the team headed back on the road, unsure if it would return to Paris again.

Opponents met the road-weary Parasites with little sympathy. Following a humiliating 21–1 loss to Corsicana, Guy Rall finally gave up on his team. Mired in debt and with shallow pockets even before he entered the baseball business, Rall briefly attempted to transfer the club to Ardmore but ultimately turned it over to the league and rejoined his friend William Miller in Fort Worth. League officials had little interest in carrying Paris and offered Billy Hughes, manager of the Enid club of the Southwestern League, control of the team; however, he showed no interest. As the Parasites continued to struggle through the worst performance of any Texas League team to date, they became a laughing stock, with opposing batters licking their chops at the thought of facing their weak pitching staff and poor fielders. Even a gift from J.W. Gardner, who agreed to relocate two mid-month games from Dallas to Fannin County, offered little help as Paris lost both in poor fashion.

In early August, with no private management secured, the league attempted to form a stock company in Paris for the purpose of operating the team. Without a guarantee it would be admitted to the league the following season, though, locals showed little interest. On August 2, following a 3–2 home loss to Corsicana, the Texas League finally transferred the Paris franchise to Ardmore, Oklahoma, its original destination, for the remainder of the season. While in Ardmore, the team's poor performance continued, with the newly named Territorians winning just three of eleven games. When the second half of the season finished, the Paris-Ardmore franchise had posted a 13-35 record, finishing twenty-seven games out of first place.

The pitiable performance of the 1904 Parasites cannot be overstated. The team finished the season with a dreadful .254 winning percentage, shutout seventeen times and outscored 569–276. Surrendering 6 runs per game, the team lost its 76 games by an average of 5.4 runs. Pitchers allowed opponents to score in excess of 10 runs twenty times during the season. Selby, Hamilton and Zook combined for only thirteen wins, with Earl Zook's 4-23 record leading the team in futility. Zook did little to help himself at the plate, batting only .130 in 49 games. The lone bright spot on the Paris team was Cy Mulkey, who won 9 games on the mound and batted .291 in his 36 games with the team. With only 29 of its 102 games played at home, however, the team's failure surprised few.

In spite of the Oilers disastrous second half, leaving them twenty and a half games behind overall leader Fort Worth, their first-half performance earned them a spot in the championship playoff series, a best-of-nineteen marathon against Fort Worth. Not content with his second-half roster heading into the championship series, Upton Blair purchased the contracts of several top players from idle teams. Fort Worth, on the other hand, stood pat with a roster having posted 72-30 record. Corsicana's strategy paid dividends as the Oilers took the championship series eleven games to eight, outscoring Fort Worth 99–68, including five shutouts.

For the third consecutive season, North Texas League officials took satisfaction in the circuit's performance. Aside from the late season relocation of the Paris franchise, the other teams finished the complete schedule in their home cities. The Fort Worth–Corsicana playoff series was generally successful, although promoters likely would have preferred if the much more talented Panthers had defeated the Oilers. Regardless, Corsicana won its second pennant in three seasons and made early plans for a third in 1905.

While the other North Texas cities appeared to have bright futures in the Texas League, disappointed Paris baseball supporters realized their city had lost the support of other league owners. Despite five seasons of effort, the Texas League had not been successful in Paris. Money was tight, fans were fickle and geography constantly placed the franchise at odds with other owners who resented the jump to the city from Dallas–Fort Worth. Likewise, the railroad difficulties in 1904 gave further credence to the argument that Paris represented an undue risk to a sustainable league. The same railroad initially encouraging John L. Ward to sweep Paris into the Texas League in 1896 became an albatross the city could not overcome. Paris never again received serious consideration as a Texas League city, but its exit allowed other growing cities a chance to win a spot on the circuit.

CHAPTER 12

1905: A SHORTER JUMP

The origins of Temple and Denison have much in common. Like Denison, Temple grew directly from the railroad. In 1873, a prairie covered the future site of Temple, and with no sizeable city to provide services, the area struggled to even sustain agriculture. All that changed, however, when Galveston businessmen proposed a new railroad bypassing Houston for points northward. The Gulf, Colorado and Santa Fe (GCSF) originated in Galveston, passed south of Houston and then turned northwestward toward Bell County, with engineers intending to lay line to Belton, the county seat.

A growing city of 1,800 residents, hotels, banks, daily mail and stagecoach service, Belton greeted the prospective railroad with enthusiasm. With the International and Great Northern Railway also approaching town, Belton made plans to become a central player in Texas commerce. By 1880, though, the city's future changed drastically when the GCSF purchased two hundred acres several miles northeast of the city for a junction where the line would split and head westward to New Mexico and northward to Fort Worth.

In 1881, Belton officials looked on with outrage as the sweeping prairie took shape as the community of Temple, named in honor of the GCSF railroad's chief engineer. Stores, restaurants, boardinghouses and schools popped up, and farmers converged on the area in anticipation of new markets for cotton and grain. By June, the GCSF began selling commercial and residential lots, and investors built quickly. The new city seemingly popped up overnight. When the Katy arrived a year later, young Temple secured its position as one of Texas's most important transportation centers. Even as county seat, the railroad arrangement in Bell County relegated Belton to second-tier status.

In 1923, the *Temple Daily Telegram* labeled the city's early days as a mixture of "pioneer spirit" and "childish ambitions and eagerness." The community grew into a rugged frontier town, but unlike other railroad towns, such as Denison, commerce didn't arrive quickly. Temple's slow-growing economy actually offered a disguised blessing as the community withstood changes that might devastate more hastily built cities. While the economy grew slowly, Temple's civic pride knew no bounds, and throughout the 1890s, city officials organized a seemingly endless array of festivals, parades and community celebrations. Temple dubbed itself "Queen City of the Prairies," a title well earned as educational and cultural resources grew rapidly.

One of Temple's greatest obstacles in building an economy did not rest with the railroad, overeager businessmen or any effort from Belton to draw commerce away from the city. Rather, Temple founders discovered a nemesis in the sticky prairie soil beneath the town. Downtown Temple became a mud pit in the rainy season, virtually impassable to wagons, with pedestrians forced to walk on wooden planks on each side of the street. For an average city, the mud and standing water may have presented health hazards from insects and disease, but Temple actually became one of Texas's healthiest cities, in no small part due to a large number of doctors and hospitals. In 1891, the GCSF constructed Temple's first hospital, a centrally located health center along the line intended to serve company employees. Soon, other hospitals opened throughout the town. Christian, Catholic, public and private hospitals all operated at one point, and in 1893, doctors outnumbered lawyers and saloons, a rarity in frontier Texas.

In 1905, the still-new Interurban Railroad revolution hit Temple when a line was constructed to Belton. The new line allowed easy transportation between Bell County's largest city and its county seat, improving services for both. Not surprisingly, the Interurban and other railroads offered Temple everything it needed to become a target for a Texas League franchise.

Initial plans for the 1905 season called for a six-team league. Again, North Texas owners decided to go it alone, remaining segregated from South Texas for another season. The central Texas cities of Austin and Waco elected to join the North Texas circuit, spreading the league geographically and limiting long jumps. With Dallas, Fort Worth and Corsicana all accepted, owners gave consideration for the final team to Sherman-Denison; Ardmore, Oklahoma; and, for the first time, Temple. The 1905 owners seemed willing to take risks, first choosing to ignore Sunday baseball prohibitions in Waco

Early Temple never missed a chance to have a celebration, and it appears most of the population is rushing to some event in this photo. *Library of Congress.*

and Corsicana, setting up a legal showdown that would impact blue laws for years to come. But the decision to locate a franchise in Temple met resistance.

League owners expressed early reservations about placing a team in Temple. The city's ballpark actually lay four miles outside town toward Belton, an inconvenient location for both players and spectators. The Interurban passed by the park, but the failure of the Sherman-Denison Interurban arrangement remained fresh in owners' minds. The young and enthusiastic Temple baseball men, though, offered to build a facility closer to town—what would later become Woodson Field—just northeast

The 1905 Temple Boll Weevils. *Authors' collection.*

of the railroad junction. League president Doak Roberts threw his support and money behind the city, leaving Corsicana in the hands of local banker C.H. Mills. Roberts proposed to establish a stock company in Temple, an arrangement still discouraged by some owners. Regardless, with Doak Roberts's involvement and his growing reputation as a baseball executive, stock sold quickly, and Temple received unanimous support of the other league owners when admitted to the Texas League in March. Texarkana officials made a last-ditch effort to secure a franchise by offering an unheard-of $5,000 entry fee, but the 220-mile jump from the nearest city made it even more financially impractical than Paris. In fact, in order to reduce expenses, league owners scheduled just four road trips per team throughout the season. While the long trips would make for weary travelers, all teams would face the same hardships as the season wore on.

When Doak Roberts arrived in Temple, he brought along the league headquarters and some of the Texas League's biggest names. Manager Ben Shelton led a team including Bill Powell, Frank Coyle, Roy Akin, Zena

Above: Boll Weevil hurler Bill Louden, 1905. *Author's collection.*

Left: Walt "Hickory" Dickson. *Author's collection.*

Roy Akin. *Author's collection.*

Clayton, Dee Poindexter, Rick Adams and Roy Mitchell. Mitchell and Adams anchored the pitching staff along with newcomers Cal Lewis and Walt "Hickory" Dickson. With Roberts's business savvy and Shelton's management, Temple established itself as the team to beat in 1905.

Though Corsicana won its second championship in three years the previous season, most of its players scattered throughout baseball when Doak Roberts left town. C.H. Mills hired manager Walter Salm to lead a club of virtual unknowns, though Tom Huddleston returned to the Oilers for another season.

Unlike previous seasons, the 1905 Corsicana squad had little impact on the league. After losing his first five games, Mills replaced Walter Salm with Irishman and former major leaguer Con Lucid. Lucid, who had once pitched and won thirty games in thirty days in the Pacific Northwestern League, offered little improvement over Salm. By the time the team faced Waco on May 17, it had won only two of twenty contests, and an impatient C.H. Mills showed Lucid the same door as his predecessor, bringing in Lou Mahaffey to manage the club. A veteran minor leaguer with brief major-league experience, Mahaffey caught a break in his debut as the Waco Navigators failed to show up for the first game of the series. By rule, Corsicana was credited with a 9–0 win. Mahaffey's magic continued to work for the next few games as the Oilers won six of seven before reverting to the performances that had cost Salm and Lucid their jobs. By June 6, mired in last place with a 10-30 record, Corsicana dropped out of the league, its spoiled fans unwilling to support a losing franchise. Other Texas League franchises picked up a few of its players who went on to moderately successful seasons, but as a team, the 1905 Corsicana Oilers were an abject failure, batting just .184 and averaging fewer than three runs per game.

While Corsicana muddled through its brief season, Ben Shelton's Temple Boll Weevils got off to an equally inauspicious start. Dubbed the "Cotton Bugs" by the *Galveston Daily News*, Temple lost nine of its first ten games before sweeping Corsicana and Fort Worth at Woodson Field. As the season wore on, the Boll Weevils had five winning streaks of six or more games. Led by Ben Shelton and Zena Clayton, by early June, the offense caught fire, and over a four-game stretch the team scored seventy-one runs on seventy-eight hits, including a 27–3 thrashing of Corsicana in which it pounded twenty-seven hits and took advantage of fourteen Corsicana errors. Temple's 14–6 victory over Corsicana on June 6 turned out to be the Oil City's final game in the Texas League. Days later, Mike O'Connor's Austin Senators also withdrew from the league, unable to sustain a fan base with their 17-22 record. Unfortunately for Mike O'Connor, it would be his last year of baseball. The Texas League original having played for virtually every Texas League city over a fifteen-year career died of tuberculosis in Austin before the 1906 season began.

The Temple Boll Weevils' 1905 success resulted from consistent inconsistency. Their several winning streaks allowed them to overcome three long losing streaks and play slightly above .500 ball from June through the end of the season. Ben Shelton led the league in six categories, including plate appearances, runs scored and hits. Third baseman Zena Clayton fared nearly as well, matching Shelton's league-leading thirty-one doubles and batting .269 while appearing in all but 6 games, second only to Shelton, who did not miss a game the entire season. Bill Powell played stellar as an unusually speedy catcher, appearing in 121 games overall and batting .266 with thirty-two stolen bases and a league-leading ten triples.

On the mound, Roy Mitchell led Temple with twenty wins in thirty-five starts, while Cal Lewis posted a 15-13 record. Rick Adams pitched only sixteen games, but his 13-3 record led the league in winning percentage and included a 5–0 no-hitter over Fort Worth on June 22. Finally, rookie Walt Dickson showed why he would eventually become a Texas League legend, sporting an 8-2 record while batting .321.

Despite their on-field prowess, the Temple Boll Weevils lost the Texas League crown to the Fort Worth Panthers and twenty-three-game-winner Harold Christman. If not for several rainouts on the season, Temple may well have won the title, but Fort Worth's schedule allowed an additional game, and its 72-59 record topped the Boll Weevils' 71-59 by just a half game. Ben Shelton, though, knew his team had its chances. A five-game losing streak over the season's last week (including four to Fort Worth) relegated the Boll Weevils to Texas League runner-up, still a substantial accomplishment for the city's first entry into the league.

Though 1905 offered the Texas League's most competitive pennant race since its 1888 founding, the season is best remembered for what happened in the courtroom. Texas's blue laws, holdovers from Puritan New England laws prohibiting recreation, commerce and other nonreligious pursuits on Sundays, became a major point of dispute during the season. Over the years, Sunday baseball created controversy throughout Texas, but baseball opponents seldom received support from enforcement officials. Those considering Sunday baseball a violation of law did occasionally force Corsicana to play outside the city limits, as in the record-breaking 1902 victory over Texarkana in Ennis. Local women's groups even tried to stop schoolboys from playing on Sundays. The boys laughed heartily at their mothers' and grandmothers' protests and played on the sandlot every Sunday afternoon. Down the road in Waco, however, local officials took their blue laws more seriously.

Waco enforced its blue laws with a vengeance, forcing Waco manager Henry Fabian to lead the challenge against Sunday baseball prohibitions. While Dallas's J.W. Gardner and others violated and occasionally paid fines for sponsoring Sunday games, Fabian took his defiance to the next level. No city in Texas seemed more opposed to Sunday baseball than Waco. In fact, its refusal to allow Sunday games had led to the city's exclusion from the Texas League on more than one occasion. Texas League franchises could not survive sitting idle for even a day. Successful baseball in Texas or any other state required relaxed blue laws.

Texas law stated, among many other prohibitions, that "places of amusement" could not legally charge admission on Sunday. Arrested three times during the 1905 season, including on July 9, when the sheriff took the entire Waco team into custody, Henry Fabian challenged the law in the courts under the pretense that the legislature adopted the statute written before baseball arrived in Texas. The law defined prohibited attractions as "places of amusement...construed to mean circuses, theaters, variety theaters, and such other amusements as are exhibited and for which a fee is charged."

Words mean things, and in the case of the law prohibiting Sunday baseball, the court's ruling hinged on the word "such." Judge Sam Scott ruled that the term "such" meant the law applied only to those amusements comparable to those specified elsewhere in the law. As the law was written before baseball existed in Texas, he noted, the word "such" did not apply to the sport, and Sunday baseball was, indeed, perfectly legal. With the court's ruling, many Texas cities relaxed their laws and allowed baseball seven days a week. Fabian became known as the "Father of Sunday Baseball" in Texas.

For several cities, Fabian's victory opened doors never before considered. New cities like Greenville and Cleburne entered the fray as competition built to acquire a 1906 franchise. The wide-open race signaled a major overhaul of the Texas League map in the coming season, and the changes would be felt for years, all the way to the major leagues.

CHAPTER 13

1906: NEW CITIES, NEW LEGENDS

Greenville and Cleburne both began as agricultural communities—Greenville thriving on row crops and Cleburne on cattle drives. Both towns struggled until the railroads arrived, but by the 1890s, rapid growth made each an important local commercial center. With both towns a short distance from Dallas and Fort Worth, it was only a matter of time before Texas League magnates took notice.

Greenville seemingly rose from the prairie. When establishing a county seat in 1846, Hunt County residents chose 640 acres of tall-grass prairie situated directly in the county's geographical center. Surveyors platted the area, and lots along the city square quickly sold. Eventually, outlying lots sold as well, and Greenville was born. Despite its political designation as county seat, Greenville was at first merely an oasis on the prairie. The area's subsistence-based agriculture offered homesteaders little reason to relocate to the city. Greenville initially offered no transportation system to support commercial farming; therefore, most of the population remained in the countryside, scratching out an existence on family farms. By the mid-1850s, community development still dragged, with only a few businesses surrounding the square.

Though Greenville grew slowly and Hunt County's population remained scattered across the countryside, education bound county residents en masse. Greenville's first school opened just a year after the community's founding, and by 1850, educators established the

Greenville, Texas, played host to the 1906 Greenville Hunters, the city's first and only franchise in the Texas League. *Courtesy Greenville Revisited.*

private Greenville Institute. During the Civil War, many Hunt County men fought with the Confederacy, and Greenville became involved in violent clashes between Rebels and Union sympathizers that carried on even after the war's end. By 1872, though, peace and growth once again returned to Greenville, and locals supported even more schools. Like Sherman, Greenville became a center of education, and when the Katy railroad arrived in 1880, the city's growth boomed. Unlike Sherman, though, Greenville didn't have to fight a nearby sister city for commerce. Throughout the 1880s, more railroad companies built through Greenville, and by the mid-1890s, six served the city. Cotton production on the fertile blackland prairie countryside grew rapidly, and commercial farming became a major economic force in Hunt County.

By 1900, Burleson College and Texas Holiness University brought higher education to Hunt County, and Greenville's population reached 8,500. The city had become one of the most important on the prairie in terms of cotton processing and a major player in all railroad commerce between Dallas, Texarkana and points beyond.

Like Greenville, Cleburne didn't start as a railroad town. About thirty miles south of Fort Worth, pioneers founded the settlement along West Buffalo Creek, a vital source of water for ranchers driving cattle herds northward along the Chisolm Trail. By 1868, the settlement became the seat of Johnson County, with a post office, newspaper and private school. Two years later, fewer than seven hundred residents inhabited Cleburne, but like the rest of North Texas, the following decade would see a population explosion.

Throughout the 1870s, the GCSF Railroad struggled to build its way from Galveston to North Texas. While other railroads followed routes leading to Dallas, the GCSF instead chose a more westward route directly to Fort Worth. Between 1879 and 1881, the railroad lay nearly three hundred miles of track connecting Fort Worth to the Gulf Coast. A year later, the GCSF purchased a line connecting Cleburne to Dallas, and the small city became a transportation crossroads.

By 1890, Cleburne's population rose to nearly four thousand as additional railroads arrived. The GCSF, though, contributed the most to Cleburne's success. By the end of the 1890s, the railroad based its machine shops in the city, and the population once again doubled to eight thousand. A few years later, no fewer than six railroads passed through the city headed to points in all directions. Like other Texas railroad communities, Cleburne's development turned the surrounding area from subsistence-based agriculture to commercial farming and ranching. For several years, corn remained the county's major crop, but by the end of the century, cotton and livestock established Cleburne as a major transportation center on the edge of the western frontier. The railroad soon replaced cattle drives to Kansas, and the Chisolm Trail gave way to the faster and more efficient rail route. With their proximity to the Dallas–Fort Worth area and easy access to points throughout Texas, both Cleburne and Greenville seemed logical choices for the Texas League's next small-city franchises.

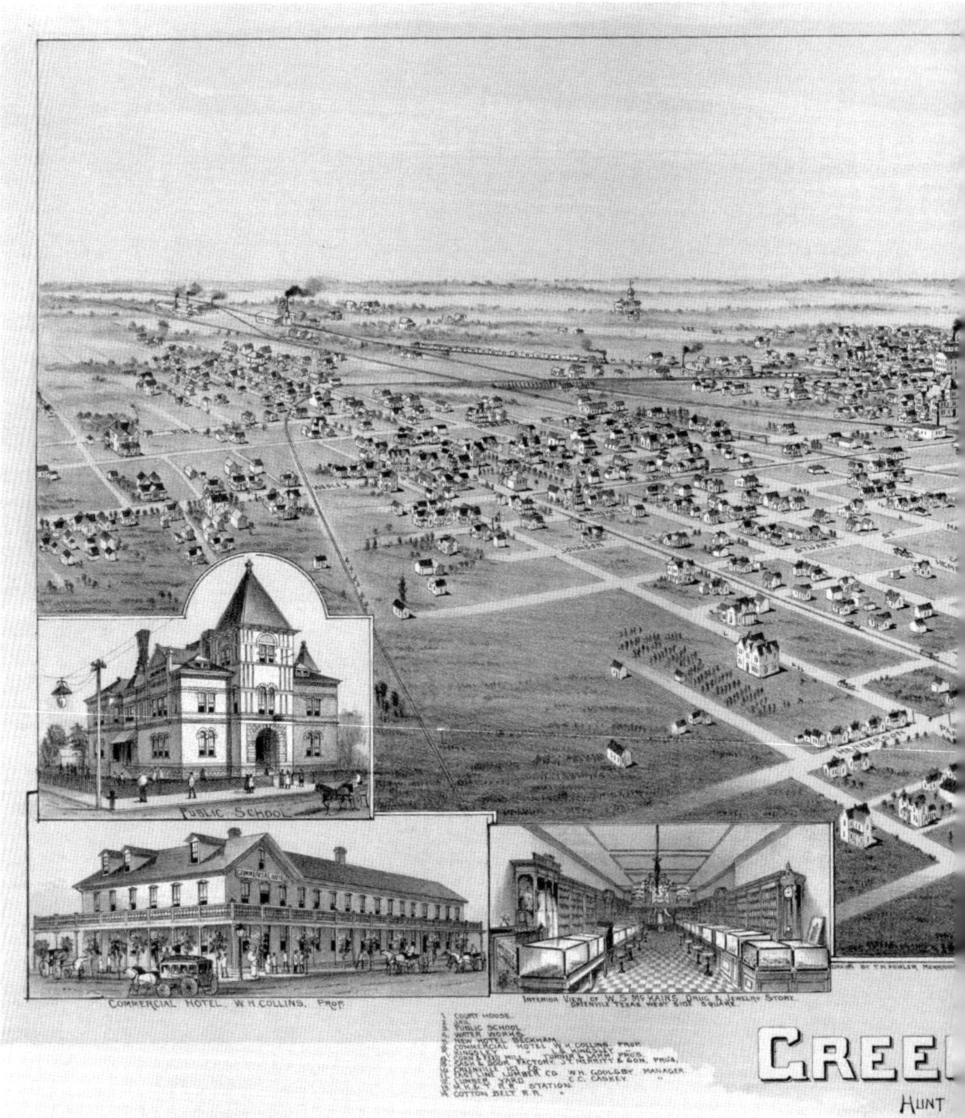

Greenville, Texas, 1891. *Courtesy Amon Carter Museum.*

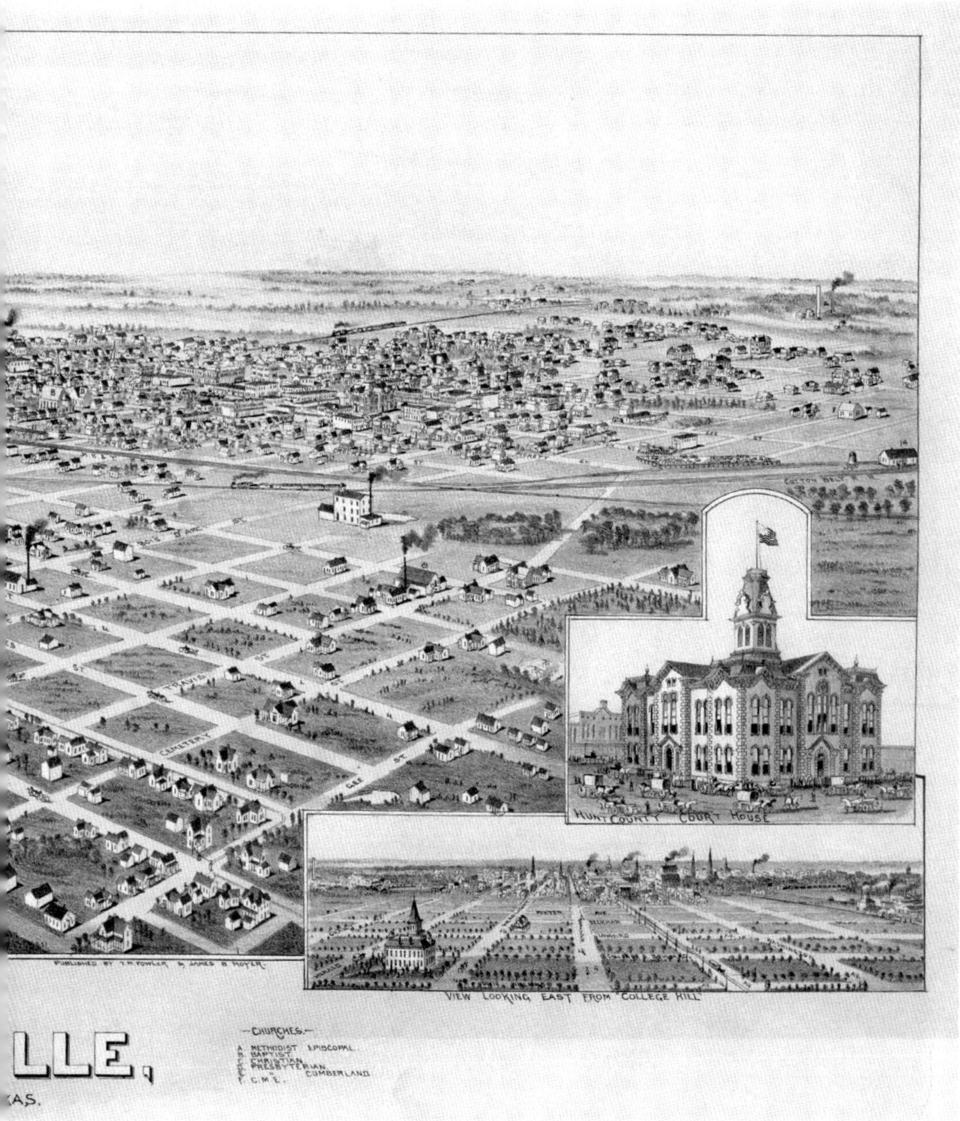
HUNT COUNTY COURT HOUSE
VIEW LOOKING EAST FROM COLLEGE HILL
PUBLISHED BY T.M. FOWLER & JAMES B. MOYER.
LLE,
XAS.
—CHURCHES.—
A. METHODIST EPISCOPAL.
B. BAPTIST.
C. CHRISTIAN.
D. PRESBYTERIAN.
E. " CUMBERLAND.
F. C.M.E.

GO TO
HARRIS & HUGHES
FOR PURE DRUGS
SOUTH SIDE SQUARE
READ-STROOP
DRUG CO.

Cleburne, Texas, circa 1900. *Library of Congress.*

Corsicana owner Doak Roberts relocated his team to Cleburne in 1906. *Courtesy Save Old Cleburne.*

While preparing for the 1906 season, Texas League owners led by Doak Roberts decided to prohibit themselves from serving as league executives. The president, often called on to set schedules, interpret player eligibility and consider protests, had to be above repute or suspicion of any wrongdoing, and someone with a vested interest in a single team did not meet the requirement. Dallas owner J.W. Gardner nominated the impartial L.D. Corbett of Paris, former secretary of the small North Texas League, to head the Texas League in 1906, and the nomination carried. Corbett immediately set about organizing a circuit, the only givens being franchises in Dallas, Fort Worth and Waco.

Over the next several months, many cities made their case for entry, or reentry, into the league. Corsicana, Sherman-Denison, Temple, Greenville, Cleburne, Texarkana and even Little Rock and Shreveport made overtures to L.D. Corbett and other league owners. As always, population, transportation and the much-heralded geographic jump between cities became the deciding factors.

Doak Roberts, never completely satisfied with any city but seemingly a fan of those to the south of Dallas–Fort Worth, visited Temple, Cleburne and Greenville to gauge public interest in a club. He found officials in Temple, the home of his very successful 1905 franchise, hesitant to support another season of baseball. Cleburne's Charles H. Thacker, though, assured Roberts that his city was ready to move forward with a ballpark and field a first-class team. Thacker held strong influence over Cleburne's affairs and had already been instrumental in establishing a lavish country club on the outskirts of town. A sporting man at heart, Thacker proved his commitment to baseball two weeks later when he organized a stock company and sold fifty shares with little effort.

By late November, both Little Rock and Shreveport dropped out of contention for a Texas League spot, electing to remain in the increasingly successful Southern League. A few days later, Charles Thacker convinced Doak Roberts of Cleburne's commitment to professional baseball, and Roberts sold his interest in the Temple franchise to local rancher and landowner John Ewing Edens. Edens, a graduate of the University of Texas, came from a wealthy family who owned large tracts of acreage south and east of Temple. His brother sat on the local bank board of directors, and Edens himself joined his brother in operating the family ranch and financial interests. With the wealthy brothers' support, others in Temple became more comfortable with a franchise and bought into Edens's stock company. The entrance of Cleburne and Temple into the league now a foregone conclusion, five of the league's six teams seemed set. Selecting these smaller cities required sacrifice on the part of owners like William H. Ward and J.W. Gardner, and they worked quickly to devise a system to support the small markets.

In order to ensure a competitive, stable league, Texas League officials offered several proposals for the 1906 season. The realization that large-market teams had to support those located in smaller cities was a major step for Ward and Gardner. After years of struggle, the two longtime owners begrudgingly accepted that teams in small cities had to remain competitive to maintain fan interest, and merely splitting the season into halves did not suffice. A new proposal called for owners to strengthen any unsuccessful small-market team through a contract-sharing system. The league instituted a loose and likely unenforceable agreement to prop up any team that fell behind in the pennant race.

By year's end, the contest for the sixth team came down to Sherman-Denison, Greenville and Texarkana. All had successfully drawn good crowds the previous season in the North Texas League, and many owners thought each ready to leap to the next level. Doak Roberts strongly supported Sherman-Denison's proposal, while Texarkana received little support, the jump from Dallas once again rearing its head. J.W. Gardner enthusiastically supported Greenville's petition, support that coupled with Gardner's opposition to salary caps and forced the league to address additional issues before the circuit could be finalized.

The issue of salary caps had been debated since professional baseball began, the Texas League no stranger to the controversy. Owners adopted salary caps for the same reason several professional sports leagues enforce them today—to maintain competitive balance, a factor ultimately in the interest of all teams involved. Early salary caps ranged from $800 to $1,200 a month, and with all league teams adhering to the same limit, a small-market team like Sherman had as much chance of signing a quality player as the more financially stable Dallas or Fort Worth franchises. Of course, crude accounting methods meant a salary cap depended on owner honesty, and "the only good salary cap is one that can be broken" became a common phrase. Indeed, many owners broke salary caps with regularity, and the unenforced cap destroyed competitive balance. Smaller towns drawing smaller crowds lost quality players to larger markets and fielded losing teams, leading to even less patronage and the eventual collapse of a franchise. With an unenforced cap, the Texas League's April circuit seldom resembled that in place at season's end.

As the 1906 season approached, Dallas Giants owner J.W. Gardner announced his opposition to continuing salary caps. During the previous season, both he and Fort Worth's W.H. Ward had broken the cap, signed quality players and played before large crowds. Gardner noted that the two franchises' success at the gate, particularly his .500 third-place Giants, proved even a team not competing for a championship could draw fans with proper promotion. To the extent of the larger markets, Gardner was probably correct. Cities like Dallas and Fort Worth could draw large crowds even when their teams failed on the field, but smaller markets had fewer hardcore kranks to support a team through lean times. Owners rebuked Gardner's efforts and agreed to both a salary cap and the new idea of sharing players when a team became uncompetitive. The concept of sharing players, though, created even more controversy.

Local owners normally operated baseball franchises. A local businessman, group of businessmen or a stock organization might apply for a franchise, sign players and run team business throughout the season. In the Texas League, though, some teams might be operated from a distance, often by an owner who held stake in more than one team in the same league. This "syndicate" arrangement created numerous controversies, particularly for a small circuit. The Texas League followed a "one team, one vote" meeting procedure. Each team had a single vote in league matters, as did the league president as tiebreaker. League owners considered democracy important to protecting the interests of all franchises, regardless of market size. In previous seasons when the league president also owned a team, the "one team, one vote" concept was jeopardized. J.W. Gardner, as he often did, led the fight against offering the extra vote when owners selected a president from among themselves. Still, no one in the Texas League was a larger proponent of syndicate baseball than Gardner himself.

Syndicate baseball undermined efforts at democracy. In a syndicate, one owner might operate two or more franchises. The "one team, one vote" arrangement remained in place, but one owner could control more than one vote. In a small league, two votes essentially allowed one owner to dominate league affairs.

In 1905, J.W. Gardner held rights to both the Dallas and Waco franchises. His two votes created controversy as other owners complained he unfairly controlled league operations, particularly those related to railroad excursion rates. Gardner often arranged low rates for excursions between Waco and Dallas, but he would not make similar arrangements for games with Corsicana, Temple or other franchises. Spectators turned out en masse for Waco-Dallas contests, and Gardner raked in all of the profits, while owners controlling only one team split gate receipts. Other league owners did not want a similar arrangement in 1906.

Greenville's H.B. Mock led the Hunt County city's effort to obtain a Texas League franchise. Mock, a baseball novice, made it well known that Greenville wanted an experienced business manager operating its club. J.W. Gardner announced that he had already been contacted by several civic leaders in Greenville and agreed to run the new franchise. Doak Roberts immediately objected, pointing out the problems of syndicate ownership. Gardner, however, insisted Waco's 1905 franchise an orphan, and he took it over not out of financial interest but rather his interest in the league as a whole. He also noted that Greenville's application for entry to the league called for a stock company, and the league had no right to restrict who could invest in such a franchise. Ultimately, Gardner lost out as the league agreed to place the franchise in H.B. Mock's name under the condition it had the right to approve stockholders. Clearly, J.W. Gardner had little chance of receiving that approval.

While J.W. Gardner fought for the right to control both his Dallas franchise and the new club in Greenville, he also pressed for the appointment of Archibald P. Bailey as league secretary. Soon after Greenville's acceptance into the league, though, Bailey inexplicably invested in the Greenville franchise, essentially removing himself from candidacy. With time short, the owners abandoned their effort to prevent a league owner from serving as its top executive, reelecting Doak Roberts as president.

Waco Baseball Association president T.W. Simpson opposed A.P. Bailey's stock purchase. Bailey, after all, was a close confidant of Gardner, and Simpson alleged that Gardner likely financed the purchase in an effort to create a secret syndicate. Simpson, a staunch supporter of the "one team, one vote" concept, convinced other owners that Gardner would dictate league affairs by obtaining multiple votes, and some owners alleged he had supported Doak Roberts as president for the very purpose of tabling the syndicate issue for the season. Indeed, Gardner did argue that Doak Roberts now had two votes, one as an owner and one as league president.

Deflecting criticism, Gardner alleged Waco's Simpson wanted cheap baseball, willing to sacrifice quality for a lower investment. Simpson countered that he had called for higher salary caps, noting that the leagues offering higher pay had been more successful financially. As it had in the early days of the Texas League, the pervasive thought that a good salary cap was one that could be broken seemed to rule the day.

Ultimately, A.P. Bailey's stock ownership in Greenville received approval, but it did not dissuade owners from believing Gardner actually called the shots from Dallas. Greenville, they believed, operated essentially as a farm club of Dallas, providing loopholes allowing Gardner to break the salary cap and ultimately buy the league championship. Gardner's true intentions can be debated, but when Greenville folded mid-season, several of its players did sign with Dallas. Then again, an equal number signed with Simpson's Waco Navigators. To this day, the complete facts of the Greenville-Dallas relationship remain a mystery.

Despite the off-season turmoil and owner disputes, owners finalized the 1906 Texas League circuit by February. Franchises in Dallas, Fort Worth, Waco and Temple welcomed new entrants Cleburne and Greenville. If the playing season held the same drama as the off-season, an eventful summer lay in store.

While no early Texas League franchise maintained a consistent roster season to season, Doak Roberts managed to resign several of his 1905 players for the move to Cleburne. Paris native Ben Shelton followed Roberts northward as manager. Infielder Mickey Coyle, also from Paris, brought his aggressive, crowd-pleasing style to Cleburne, along with a remarkable ability to drive the ball despite his right hand having been mangled in an accident. Stocky third baseman and eventual fourteen-year minor leaguer Roy Akin signed with Cleburne as well, as did catcher Bill Powell and outfielder Dee Poindexter from neighboring Ellis County. A third Parisian, Rick Adams, anchored a pitching staff that included Dode Criss and second-year hurler Walt Dickson, who Doak Roberts expected to have a breakout season. Roberts also signed George "Lucky" Whiteman, an outfielder who earned his nickname by playing on a number of championship teams during his career. Originally a diving acrobat, Whiteman chose the less dangerous sport of baseball when his partner died in a performance. The move proved lucrative as Whiteman went on to play over 3,200 games in twenty-four seasons of minor-league baseball, as well as three seasons in the major leagues. In fact, many credit Whiteman as the unsung hero of the 1918 World Series because, while playing for Boston, he had several clutch hits and fielding plays. Notorious hothead Parker Arbogast and former St. Louis Cardinal Charlie Moran rounded out Cleburne's opening day roster.

When Roberts carried a large portion of his team northward, J.E. Edens was left to scrape together a team in Temple. Major-league veteran Con Lucid signed on as manager, while Otto Frederick, Fred Moore, Hugh McCulley and Bill Yoke made up the infield. Error-prone Walt Pease, light-hitting F.W. Sullinger and William Butler joined the outfield, and Neal

Texas Leaguer, college football coach and Major League umpire "Uncle" Charley Moran. *Author's collection.*

Dode Criss, noted by Ty Cobb as one of the best pure hitters he had ever seen. *Author's collection.*

Vance handled most of the pitching duties along with an occasional pitcher Edens signed for a game or two during the season.

The 1906 Boll Weevils did not claim experience as a strong point. With the exception of Bill Yoke, who had a long minor-league career, appeared briefly in the majors and later became a manager, none of Edens's signees had played more than five years of professional baseball. Most of the Temple roster played a few years in the Texas League before retiring to occupations as bricklayers, chemists, farmers and postmen.

While Edens struggled to sign players, A.P. Bailey had far less trouble in Greenville, with or without the help of J.W. Gardner. Soon after obtaining the franchise, Bailey named Don Curtis field manager. While not an outstanding ballplayer in his six minor-league seasons, Curtis had an eye for talent. He later parlayed into a successful career as a major-league scout, where he discovered pitcher Dizzy Dean for the St. Louis Cardinals. When assembling his Greenville franchise, Curtis didn't have access to Hall of Fame–caliber talent, but he did bring in some veterans to put together a formidable lineup.

Greenville's infield consisted of workhorses J.D. Raley, rookies W.E. Snedden and Henry Maag and future major leaguer Bill Louden. Outfielders included Curtis, sixteen-year minor leaguer Otto McIvor and W.R. Jackson. The pitching staff consisted primarily of the towering six-foot-four Frank Moore and converted outfielder Billy Doyle. Of those on the roster, Billy Doyle had the strongest connection to J.W. Gardner, having played remarkably well in the Dallas outfield the previous three seasons. Likewise, Don Curtis and Otto McIver previously played in Dallas, and Curtis undoubtedly stayed in close touch with Gardner either personally or through A.P. Bailey. In

Future major leaguer Bill Louden. *Author's collection.*

fact, by mid-season, most of the Greenville infield found itself playing in Dallas's Gaston Park, while several others, including Billy Doyle, signed with Waco. Attesting to Don Curtis's eye for talent, several of his signings went on to long professional careers in both the minor and major leagues.

Cleburne's 1906 campaign nearly derailed before the season even opened. On April 12, during the seventh inning of an exhibition contest with the South Texas League's San Antonio franchise, a major storm hit the Railroaders' newly built ballpark. Although not a tornado, the storm destroyed crops and damaged numerous structures in and around Cleburne, not the least of which was the new grandstand, packed with fans at the time. The grandstand collapse severely injured one spectator, and he died a few days later. While the rest of the community assessed the damage, within hours, a group of fifty workers began reconstructing the grandstand. Within a matter of days, the ballpark was once again new and ready for the season opener on April 25.

Greenville, Cleburne and Temple all opened the 1906 season at home. Temple retained its Boll Weevils nickname, and the newspapers continued to modify it to the "Cotton Bugs" with glee. Cleburne took the moniker of the Railroaders, a tribute to the growing influence of the railroad on the community. Greenville, the largest city in Hunt County, dubbed itself the Hunters. They donned uniforms with the primary color being, of course, hunter green. Dallas and Fort Worth remained the Giants and Panthers, respectively, while the Navigators made their home in Waco.

Of the three small-city franchises, Greenville got off to the best start, sweeping Fort Worth in three games and then taking the first of a three-game series in Dallas before being shut out in the remaining contests. Temple started nearly as well, taking two of three from Waco at home before losing two of three against the Navigators on the road. The powerful Cleburne lineup, on the other hand, had far less success, starting the season with six consecutive losses to Dallas and Fort Worth. By the end of the season's first week, Dallas sat in first place with Cleburne bringing up the rear, already five games back.

While 1906 allowed spectators in new cities to see professional baseball, it also brought innovation. The Western Union telegraph system partnered with the Texas League to transmit scores between cities every three innings, and for the first time, baseball enthusiasts no longer had to wait until the next day's newspaper to find out where the home team stood in the standings. In 1906, a single man with a telegraph machine and a bullhorn served as the twenty-first century's multimillion-dollar high-definition scoreboard. But for die-hard baseball kranks, the innovation was a major step forward.

As the season moved into May, Greenville and Temple continued to play .500 ball, but Cleburne's fortunes changed for the better. Opening the month winning four of five from Waco and Dallas, the Railroaders began to rise in the standings. Doak Roberts, however, already saw trouble on the horizon. The team's poor start, coupled with rainy weather, postponements and the city's rebuilding from the April storms, hampered attendance. Roberts expressed concern to longtime friend Charles Thacker that Cleburne may not be cut out to support professional baseball. Roberts announced intentions to relocate the team to his hometown of Corsicana, a proven baseball market.

Roberts's plan outraged Cleburne officials. Mayor Phil Allin and the Cleburne Baseball Association informed Roberts under the threat of a lawsuit that they had invested $1,500 in the ballpark he demanded to attract the team and had already rebuilt it on a moment's notice. Likewise, Allin pointed out that several attractions, including a circus and carnival, competed with baseball for early season patronage and that the poor weather had an uncontrollable negative impact. In the meantime, both Corsicana and Texarkana courted Roberts's club.

In an effort to appease local officials, Roberts agreed to play three additional games in Cleburne as a test of viability. Roberts did not deny that the ball club had its supporters; however, he remained unconvinced that Cleburne offered enough community enthusiasm to make the venture profitable. By May 13, Roberts insisted he had lost too much money to continue, and many suspected that his wife, who cared little for her husband's baseball obsession, preferred he resume his career as a Corsicana merchant.

Roberts informed the Baseball Association that his franchise needed gate receipts of $105 per game to break even, and through the team's first eight home games, he had netted a loss of $190. With relocation of the franchise an increasing possibility, the Cleburne Baseball Association made the bold agreement to guarantee Doak Roberts against any losses if he kept the team in the city for the entire season. To Mrs. Roberts's dismay, her husband agreed to the proposal, setting the stage for some of the most interesting developments in the Texas League to date.

As Temple began to sink in the standings and Con Lucid gave up his managing duties, owner J.E. Edens searched for a way out of the league. Rumors of Cleburne relocating to Temple arose, but this time, Doak Roberts outright denied them, noting that Cleburne had become an enthusiastic baseball town. Meanwhile, Edens arranged to sell the Boll Weevils to a stock company headed by Fred Hamill. Stockholders invested over $3,000 in the team, seemingly securing its spot for the remainder of the season. With Fred Moore as new manager, by the end of May, the Boll Weevils sat in fifth place with a 14-21 record, trailed only by Waco.

A month into the season, Dallas sportswriters offered an assessment of the league. As expected, Dallas and Fort Worth led all teams, with Greenville surprisingly holding third place. Writers noted the Hunters as the best-fielding team in the league but without any pitching support. Temple, they wrote, could not hit, while Cleburne was a brutal disappointment. Waco went unmentioned, its .265 winning percentage hardly worthy of column space.

While Greenville appeared to hold its own in its inaugural season, by early June, the Hunters showed signs of disorganization. The league fined the Hunters fifty dollars after the team reportedly missed a Dallas rail connection and failed to show for its June 6 game at Cleburne. With fifty dollars being a hefty fine, Greenville sought a court injunction, eroding support for the franchise among other owners. In an attempt to deflect criticism, A.P. Bailey accused Temple of failing to pay Greenville its standard guarantee, and with the recent transfer of the Boll Weevils to a stock company, it appeared both teams stood on shaky financial ground.

While Temple and Greenville squabbled over a total of $100, on-field play continued. Dallas and Fort Worth led the league through June, with owners deciding mid-month to divide the season to maintain fan interest in the remaining clubs. As the end of the month neared, discussions of dropping two franchises for the second half grew louder, with Greenville and Temple the most likely victims. Unsurprisingly, Greenville put up little fight and prepared to transfer its players to Dallas and Waco, its most notable achievement in the Texas League being Farmer Moore's 1–0 no-hitter against Cleburne on May 8. Temple, on the other hand, threatened the league with a lawsuit. Having just invested $3,000 in the franchise, the Temple Baseball Association sought an injunction against the league and retained local lawyer J.H. Sullivan to represent them. Regardless, on July 4, with the league officially having dropped the franchise, Temple released its players, several of whom signed on with other franchises.

The mid-season departure of Greenville and Temple created tension within the Texas League. Greenville's passive reaction to the loss of its team and J.W. Gardner's frustration with the Giants' second-place finish in the season's first half offered circumstantial proof to many that Greenville had indeed been merely a stockyard for Gardner's talent. Meanwhile, as anger increased in Temple, Doak Roberts offered to move a few of his home games to the city. His offer, however sincere it may have been, did little to diminish Temple's frustration. The association eventually filed a formal suit against the league, requesting an accounting of its finances, future prohibition against unilateral franchise contraction and an admission on the league's behalf that it illegally abandoned Temple when Greenville left the league. In essence, the Temple Baseball Association demanded reformation of Texas League operations, claiming an injustice to both the team and its citizens. In late August, Judge Marshall Surratt ruled the league itself not liable for any damages Temple may have suffered but noted that the owners could be liable as individuals.

As the league found itself embroiled in controversy, few took notice when Doak Roberts traveled to Hubbard, Texas, to scout the local talent. Although Roberts had his eye on an outfielder, Hubbard's left-handed pitcher and local farm boy Tristam Speaker stood out. At game's end, Roberts asked the youngster if he'd be interested in playing professional ball, promising to return in two weeks with a contract. As promised, on his way to Waco, Roberts stopped off at Hubbard and handed Speaker one dollar for rail fare to the city, expecting him to arrive well before Cleburne's game against the Navigators. Rather than waste the dollar on travel expenses, Speaker pocketed the money, hopped a freight car to Waco and showed up just in time for the ballgame.

Despite Doak Roberts's signing of Speaker and his authority as owner, Cleburne manager Ben Shelton did not take a quick liking to the youngster. "Gentlemen" Ben, known throughout baseball for his even temperament under even the worst circumstances, became angered with Speaker's late arrival to his first game but nonetheless placed him on the mound. Though the Railroader's lost to Waco 3–0, Speaker's pitching drew rave reviews as he allowed only four hits.

With Ben Shelton still angry with his new pitcher, Mickey Coyle stepped in as mediator when Roberts and Shelton met to discuss Speaker's future with the franchise. Coyle defended Shelton, noting that the "kid" had already cussed out the unflappable manager and challenged every member of the team to a fistfight. Roberts set off in search of Speaker, finding him at a local hotel. When confronted, Speaker did not deny insulting Shelton, noting he was a "splay-footed, butterfingered tramp who ought to pay his way into the ballpark." He likewise insulted Coyle, the "monkey-faced second baseman."

Doak Roberts found himself in a bind. Players, umpires, sportswriters and fans alike loved Ben Shelton. Tris Speaker, on the other hand, was a raw talent who had managed to outrage an entire team in just one day. Roberts could only imagine what would happen to his Railroaders as word of Speaker's temper spread throughout the league, but he knew he couldn't afford to lose out on his talent. A few years earlier, Roberts had turned down an offer to purchase up-and-coming Detroit Tigers star Ty Cobb, and he simply was not willing to pass on the opportunity to sign Speaker. If Roberts knew talent as well as he'd shown in previous seasons, Tris Speaker would put Texas on the map of all scouts, and the ramifications for the Texas League and Texas baseball in general would be enormous. So Roberts set out to broker a deal between his manager and new pitcher.

In exchange for a formal apology to Ben Shelton, Roberts offered Speaker a fifty-dollar-a-month contract to play for the Railroaders. Though reluctant to admit any fault, Speaker agreed and offered his apology. "Gentleman" Ben may have forgiven his new pitcher, but he certainly did not forget. In his next few appearances on the mound, Shelton left Speaker in despite being totally ineffective and allowing the opposition to spray hits around the field at will. Before one game, as he watched Speaker chase down fly balls during warm-ups, Shelton realized he had not a pitcher but a natural outfielder on his hands. With some tutoring, Speaker held the potential to be among baseball's finest. Shelton assigned Curley Maloney as Speaker's personal mentor and, as the season wore on, converted him to a full-time outfielder. While his first season wasn't stellar, Speaker did bat .268 and steal thirty-three bases in eighty-four games. His 2-7 pitching record became merely a footnote to history.

Tris Speaker's 1906 season raised a few eyebrows within the league, and Doak Roberts's discovery of the eighteen-year-old, Ben Shelton's recognition

Hubbard, Texas native and National Baseball Hall of Fame member Tris Speaker. *Author's collection.*

of him as an outfielder rather than a pitcher and Curley Maloney's coaching brought attention to the Texas League. Since the league's founding in 1888, most had considered it a destination for second-rate ballplayers. Few of the league's top players claimed Texas as home, and even fewer went on to the major leagues. By 1907, though, when Tris Speaker followed Doak Roberts to the Houston franchise, all baseball took notice. Speaker's .314 batting average led the league, as did his thirty-two doubles and twelve triples. He topped his 1906 stolen base total with thirty-six and drew interest from major-league teams as the season wore along. Roberts shopped his prospect around, first ignored by the St. Louis Browns and then turned down by the Pittsburgh Pirates because Speaker smoked cigarettes. Eventually, the Boston Red Sox purchased Speaker for an amount less than $1,000. Like Tony Thebo, though, Tris Speaker had to overcome the objections of his mother, who much preferred he stay home and enter the cattle business. Fortunately for Texas and baseball history, Mrs. Speaker relented, and Tris Speaker remains atop the list of the greatest outfielders to ever play in the major leagues.

Despite his signing of Tris Speaker, Doak Roberts realized that the Railroaders had fallen short in the first half of the 1906 season and would have to step up their play if they were to face champion Fort Worth in a playoff series for the pennant. After starting the second half losing seven of eight games, the Railroaders caught fire, led by pitchers Rick Adams, Walt Dickson and Dode Criss. Cleburne carried the second half of the season based on its outstanding pitching, including no-hitters from Adams and Dickson. Winning streaks of six, six and five games kept the Railroaders in the hunt for the second-half title as the season reached its final day.

To wrap up the season, Walt Dickson pitched both ends of a double-header at Fort Worth, allowing just six hits in each game. Cleburne won both by identical scores of 2–0, taking the second-half crown. Dickson's double-header shutout remains one of the Texas League's most historic performances. Although league rules called for a playoff between Fort Worth and Cleburne, following a rainout on the season's final day, Fort Worth's roster disintegrated as players left the city or signed with independent teams elsewhere. Rumors persisted that the Panthers' performance on the season's last day discouraged them from challenging the Railroaders again. The playoff series apparently cancelled, Cleburne soon dismantled its team as well. The Texas League declared Cleburne champion based on Fort Worth's "forfeit" of the playoff series, but Cleburne had little time to celebrate. By September 7, Doak Roberts settled with the Cleburne Baseball Association and its guarantee against loss, and the Railroaders left town. Though Cleburne claimed its pennant, 1906 represented the city's only appearance in the Texas League, and the city remains the only one to claim a championship in its only season.

Although the Texas League struggled with off-field issues for the second consecutive season, overall, the 1906 season was again a success. Games in Fort Worth and Dallas drew large crowds, and the success of those two franchises normally served as a gauge for the league as a whole. Yet league president Doak Roberts remained concerned for the sustainability of baseball in the state. For the past several seasons, Texas baseball had been divided into two distinct leagues: North Texas and South Texas. Of the two, the South Texas League was arguably the more successful. During the four seasons of the South Texas League, only one franchise did not complete its full schedule, and the league secured a Class C designation, a step up from the North Texas League's Class D standing. Doak Roberts knew that if the two leagues could merge and build upon the South Texas League's success, a strong statewide league would finally be possible.

CHAPTER 14

1907: THE SMALL MARKET'S LAST STAND

Before the outfield grass began growing in Texas League ballparks, negotiations swung into gear for 1907. Owners in both North and South Texas expressed interest in reuniting, although hard feelings between the groups still existed. During the previous four seasons, owners in both leagues accused the others of stealing their players away mid-season for higher contracts. As players of the early Texas League had little allegiance to a given city and no allegiance whatsoever to an owner, they quickly jumped franchises at the sight of a higher-paying contract. Any reunification between the leagues would require this practice to come to an end.

Soon after discussions of a statewide league began, J.W. Gardner once again reared his bombastic rhetoric. He noted that North Texas owners were tired of being forced to carry more than one team, alluding to the larger cities propping up smaller markets as the season wore on. Once again, he chided those who opposed syndicate baseball, leading to further questions about his relationship with Greenville in 1906. By late October, Gardner declared the reunification dead, expecting a six-team North Texas League for 1907. The remaining owners, however, lacked Gardner's pessimism and worked to get a deal completed.

Once convincing Gardner of reunification's benefits, the makeup of the 1907 Texas League, unlike previous seasons, was largely set. Defending South Texas League champion Austin would remain in the Southern Division, along with San Antonio, Galveston and Houston. The North would include Dallas, Fort Worth and Waco, with Temple or Cleburne to be selected for the final spot.

While Temple had been dropped from the 1906 circuit, the owners considered it a better baseball town than Cleburne. Doak Roberts had many problems attracting enough fans to watch his champion Cleburne Railroaders, and with South Texas once again involved, Temple made for an easier jump geographically. Officials, though, had to overcome one obstacle—Temple's still undecided lawsuit against the 1906 owners for abandoning the team just a few months earlier.

Aside from the lawsuit, Temple supporters still met their invitation with hesitance. The $5,000 guarantee required from each team represented the highest franchise fee to date. Temple fully understood it could not be profitable among cities like Dallas, Fort Worth, San Antonio and Houston without firm rules in place, specifically a reasonable, enforced salary cap.

Temple's demands placed salary cap opponent J.W. Gardner in a bind. He insisted Texans would not support a four-team "bush league," with eight teams needed to compete. If not Temple, options included Cleburne, Beaumont and Lake Charles, Louisiana. For purposes of the jump, though, Gardner knew Temple represented the only suitable location for a statewide league.

Negotiations stalling, by December, Temple threatened to form another league with Tyler, Waco, Hillsboro and Texarkana. With Doak Roberts having moved on to organize the Houston franchise, Temple remained without an experienced leader, and as 1906 came to an end, Temple's willingness or ability to join the league remained in question.

If a poll of early twentieth-century Texas League ballplayers had been taken, Ben Shelton would likely have ranked among the shrewdest and most likeable men in the league. A native of Alabama, Shelton's family moved to Paris in the early 1890s, at which point his father entered North Texas's growing cotton industry. A few years later, Shelton ranked among the best ballplayers in Lamar County and had taken up with Tony Thebo, another Paris baseball prodigy three years his junior. Shelton taught Thebo the finer points of hitting and fielding, but he offered little advice in the area of baserunning, the strongest part of Thebo's game and a skill Shelton would not forget in later years.

Teams all over Texas sought the services of the likeable Ben Shelton, known as both "Gentleman Ben" and "Prince Ben" for his congenial and refined personality. After beginning his professional career in South Texas in 1899, Shelton moved northward, playing in the Pacific Northwest, Montana

State and Three-I Leagues over the next three seasons. By 1903, though, Ben readied to return to his adopted home state, where the reorganized Texas League showed signs of stability.

Many baseball aficionados believe the most average players make the best coaches. Most superstars and record holders are born with natural talent and come by success with relative ease. To the contrary, the average player has to learn the nuances of the game, refine his techniques and continually adjust to the many situations he might face over the course of a baseball season. The average player spends his career as a student of the game, and those who have studied the sport naturally become the best teachers. When it came to baseball, few studied as hard as Ben Shelton.

In his early years as a professional, Shelton was a rather poor fielder and below-average batsman. However, his return to Texas in 1903 and subsequent signing with the defending champion Corsicana Oil Citys signaled a shift in Shelton's fortunes. His batting average improved to .296 over sixty-seven games, followed by a brief stint with Pine Bluff of the Cotton States League in which he batted .440. In 1904, he left North Texas for Galveston, batting .351 before rejoining Corsicana and maintaining one of the highest batting averages in all of Texas.

By 1906, Shelton's playing and coaching abilities impressed Doak Roberts to the point that he selected "Gentleman Ben" to head his new Cleburne franchise. Shelton went on to lead the Railroaders to the pennant, discovering Tris Speaker's unmatched abilities in the outfield and helping shape the rambunctious youngster into a team player.

With the 1907 Texas League still short a city and an owner in early January, Ben Shelton's reputation headed discussions among league officials. Temple organizers demanded a team leader of impeccable character and confidence, as well as a guarantee that the city would not again be dropped from the league. In Doak Roberts's mind, one man fit the bill. He wired Shelton at his home in Terrell, where Ben had followed in his father's footsteps and entered the cotton business. Roberts convinced Shelton to catch the next train to Dallas to meet with league officials. Upon arrival, Shelton stood ready for the league's offer. Still, he knew the league needed him more than he needed it, and he brought his own list of demands to the table.

Shelton insisted that if he was going to associate himself with a team, he would settle for nothing less than a first-rate ball club. Other owners agreed to offer Shelton one or two players from their rosters to assist him in assembling a competitive team. Still, Shelton wasn't satisfied. He demanded his pick of those players. He wanted no castoffs. The league reluctantly accepted

Shelton's demands, and he then went about choosing between Cleburne and Temple as a home for his franchise. Lack of organization and enthusiasm in Cleburne led him southward, where he met with Temple officials.

Shelton's control of the eighth franchise boosted Temple supporters' confidence. League owners would surely support Gentleman Ben in any endeavor, and they agreed to form a stock company if the league would settle the previous season's lawsuit. But as they were being held liable as individuals, owners remained reluctant to settle out of court. Shelton and his personable demeanor, however, won the day. He convinced Temple to proceed in spite of the suit and, by the end of January, busily assembled his team.

With only ten weeks until the scheduled season opening, Shelton knew he had little time to sign players. His first choice, Tris Speaker's mentor Curley Maloney, had already signed with Dallas, and Speaker himself had followed Doak Roberts to Houston. Still, Shelton secured the services of well-known names like Mickey Coyle, Harry Longley, Otto McIvor, Zena Clayton, Nig Ragsdale, Dee Poindexter and longtime friend Tony Thebo. His pitching staff of Billy Doyle, Jack Jarvis and Roy McFarland had experienced only moderate success over their short careers, but Shelton knew he could rely on a powerful offense and excellent fielding if his pitching faltered. As opening day neared, baseball kranks raved over the team Shelton had assembled, and Temple bragged that its Boll Weevils would be the class of the league.

All Texas League owners knew the success of a statewide league required proven leadership and cooperation between the formerly separate leagues. While Doak Roberts remained a favorite in North Texas, the league instead elected former South Texas League president Dr. William Robbie as its president for 1907. Though embroiled in a controversy with the State Board of Medical Examiners over his license to practice in the state, Robbie's success, particularly his ability to upgrade the South Texas League's to a "C" classification, impressed all, and even Roberts himself threw Robbie his support. With the league finally reunified and leadership in place, officials drew up an ambitious 140-game schedule with no plans for a split season.

Before the season even began, Temple again became the subject of controversy. Reporters insisted William Robbie remained unconvinced of Temple's ability to finish out the season and had already been in contact with Beaumont officials should the Boll Weevils falter. Robbie, though, vehemently denied any contact with Beaumont, and the rumors quickly passed. Beaumont and Lake Charles, Louisiana, both former South Texas League members, would receive no invitation to join the new Texas League, one which officials at both the league and team level expected to be a rousing success.

Dr. William Robbie, 1907 Texas League president. *Author's collection.*

Temple's ballpark sat on the northwest corner of town, abutting the growing rail yard. With streetcar service extending to the area from downtown, spectators still had to walk nearly a quarter of a mile to the ball field after disembarking. The walking distance concerned Ben Shelton from a promotion standpoint, but he stood confident that a competitive team remaining in the pennant race throughout the season would be able to draw fans despite the minor inconvenience.

With Ben Shelton's virtual free reign to design the club he wanted, few questioned Temple's ability to remain in, if not lead, the pennant race. After an opening day loss at Galveston, the Boll Weevils went on to post two consecutive shutouts before playing five consecutive one-run games. Their 1-4 record in those games was far from the outcome Ben Shelton may have wanted, but his pitching staff weathered the games at Houston and San Antonio well. In fact, during the season's first eight games, Temple pitching surrendered a total of only fourteen runs. The team's perceived offensive strength, though, had shown itself only once in an 11–0 win over Galveston. Aside from the lopsided victory, Boll Weevils hitters managed only twelve runs to begin the young season.

Heavy rains plagued Central Texas in early May. The rain reduced Temple streets to the sticky mud it had become famous for, and half the Boll Weevils' first eight home games were rainouts, including an entire series against Austin. By the time the team headed back on the road, it had split its home games, entering mid-May with a mediocre 8-10 record. The promising offense had still not hit stride, with most games low-scoring affairs. The pitching remained a surprise, holding Shelton's club in most games as it awaited offensive support.

Temple experienced success on its next road trip to Fort Worth and Dallas as the offense began to click. The team returned home to another rainout and four consecutive wins over Fort Worth and Austin, resulting in the season's longest winning streak of six games. Still, the Boll Weevils heralded lineup never caught fire. A few times over the course of the season, the offense broke open, scoring ten or more runs a total of twelve times, including a twenty-three-run outburst against Galveston on June 30. But in the early 1900s, high-scoring games were common, and twelve- or ten-run games were not extraordinary. The pitching staff, however, equaled the offensive success, allowing ten or more runs itself on only twelve occasions and recording five shutouts.

Despite any winning streaks, offensive outbursts or great pitching performances, the fate of Temple's 1907 success rested on one statistic: the Boll Weevil offense, which featured some of the strongest batters and fastest base runners of its time, found itself shut out twenty-four times over the course of the season, a rate of nearly one shutout in every five games. Suffering losing streaks of seven and eleven games, as well as two of nine games, the Boll Weevils found themselves out of competition for the first-half pennant long before it ended and never offered themselves a chance in the season's second half. By the end of July, the Boll Weevils had essentially quit on the affable Ben Shelton and punctuated their disappointing season by scoring a total of one run over five games at Dallas and Fort Worth, including four consecutive shutouts in the season's next-to-last week. The team's performance brought gate receipts to a mere trickle, and in order to survive financially, Ben Shelton moved his team on the road for the remainder of the season.

Temple's 51-87 record rated dead last in the Texas League, a full thirty-six games behind the pennant-winning Austin Senators. The Boll Weevils' promising start in Temple in 1905 only a distant memory, rooters had suffered consecutive last-place finishes, including the frustration of being dropped from the 1906 circuit mid-season.

From the standpoint of individual statistics, the Boll Weevils fared little better than the team as a whole. Roy McFarland did lead the team to twenty-one wins on the mound, followed by William Jarvis's fifteen. But highly touted Billy Doyle managed just an 8-28 record and led the league in losses. Likewise, Doyle failed miserably at the plate, batting only .183 with just seven extra-base hits.

Offensively, only Otto McIvor batted over .300, but he played in only half the season's games. Aside from McIvor, only Foley White and Tony Thebo batted over .250, with Thebo the team's iron man, appearing in all but six games and stealing thirty-five bases. Along the way, Ben Shelton tried to pick up a spare player here and there, but none met with any success, most not even batting .200 and leaving the team after just a few games.

Despite Temple's failure in 1907, league owners regarded the reunification of the Texas League as a success. All eight teams finished the season in their original cities, the full 140-game schedule played to completion. Tris Speaker finished his second and last Texas League season leading the league in batting average, doubles and triples. By season's end, Speaker had moved on to the major leagues, where he would remain for the next twenty-two seasons. Arguably the Texas League's most famous and successful alumnus, Speaker's career ended with his election to the National Baseball Hall of Fame in 1937, based on his lifetime .344 batting average and unsurpassed defensive play.

For Temple, 1907 marked its last entry into the Texas League. As Ben Shelton feared at the season's beginning, Temple baseball enthusiasts only made the long trek to the ballpark to support a winning team, and at no point during the year did the Boll Weevils give any indication they would make a run at the pennant. Likewise, the community remained angry at the league regarding its 1906 treatment and found itself unwillingly to support Texas League efforts even at the expense of its own struggling franchise. Though Shelton still thought Temple to be a baseball town, he showed no interest in returning his franchise to the city for another season and recommended city leaders either relocate the ballpark or extend the streetcar lines if they expected another investor to come to town. Soon after season's end, Shelton sold interests in the Boll Weevils to Shreveport investors, and in future seasons, the Texas League spread beyond the Lone Star State.

AFTERWORD

Following the 1907 season, the reunified Texas League experienced continued success. With eight-team circuits virtually guaranteed each season and the old stalwarts of Dallas, Fort Worth, Houston, San Antonio, Austin, Galveston and Waco finally growing in population to the point they could easily sustain Texas League franchises on a yearly basis, the need for the smaller cities of North Texas to fill out the league had diminished. Sherman, Denison, Paris, Corsicana, Cleburne, Temple, Greenville and Texarkana remained second-tier cities, and as the Texas League grew in national stature, they could no longer support high-level minor-league baseball. Furthermore, the famous "jump," a hindrance to several cities both large and small over the Texas League's first two decades, had been rendered meaningless by competitive statewide rail service, affordable travel, better adherence to schedules and increased ability of team owners to promote special excursions for fans who wanted to follow their teams between cities.

Though the second-tier cities never again found a home in the Texas League, professional baseball in the communities did not die. Sherman and Denison went on to field a number of joint teams in several leagues before and after World War II, and Paris fielded low-level professional ball clubs sporadically until the war, with a steady stream of teams in the Big State League, Sooner League and Texas-Oklahoma League until 1957. Cleburne followed its 1906 championship season with entrants in three additional leagues over four seasons. Likewise, Temple fielded several teams throughout the early and mid-twentieth century in circuits like the Middle Texas,

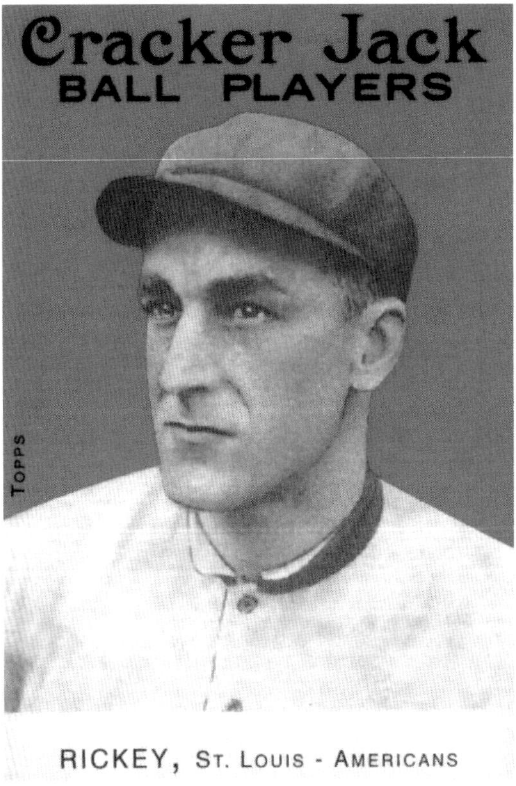

Above: Historic Majors Field Entrance, Greenville, Texas. *Karen Rutherford photo*.

Left: Hall of Famer Branch Rickey broke baseball's color barrier with the signing of Jackie Robinson, but long before he worked in the Brooklyn Dodgers front office, he played Texas League Baseball. *Author's collection*.

Central Texas and Big State Leagues. Finally, Greenville and Texarkana, two cities with the shortest tenure of any Texas League team, found little difficulty filling the stands for games in the low-level minors. In fact, in 1946, Greenville set a Class C record when over 160,000 fans attended games in historic Majors Field.

While the cities that hosted them may have been forgotten, some of the players and feats that took place in these communities remain part of Texas League lore. From Corsicana's 51–3 beatdown of Texarkana to "Hickory" Dickson's season-ending double-header shutout to claim Cleburne's 1906 championship, both history books and the Internet are filled with references to the early Texas League's achievements. Texas League Hall of Famers "Big" Mike O'Connor, Clyde Bateman, J. Doak Roberts, Tris Speaker and Wilson Matthews all played important roles in the early Texas League cities, and some—including Speaker and Branch Rickey—took their on and off-field talents all the way to the National Baseball Hall of Fame. Tony Thebo's ninety stolen bases in 1908 remain a "modern" Texas League record, as does Lucky Wright's thirty-five wins for Corsicana in 1902. Likewise, the 1902 Oil City team's .796 winning percentage remains a league best, and the team has often been mentioned as one of minor-league baseball's finest. On the other end of the spectrum, Miller and Rall's 1904 Paris entry's .255 winning percentage remains one of the worst in minor-league history.

Well into the twenty-first century, most Texas League followers have long forgotten the early cities forged from the prairie that helped hold the league

By 1910, Corsicana's early ball field had been replaced by this park, complete with covered grandstand. *Courtesy Ron Maxfield.*

together in its most trying years. Over the seasons, cities like Amarillo, El Paso, Tyler and Beaumont have all had their crack at Texas League franchises, and when Major League Baseball arrived in the state in the early 1960s and '70s, franchises in Dallas, Fort Worth, Houston and Galveston folded or lost large portions of their fan base in favor of big-league ball. Although the league officials had dabbled with cities around the state over the years, by 2010, Texas League teams had been based in Oklahoma, Kansas, Arkansas, Louisiana, New Mexico, Missouri and even Tennessee. Many seasons found only half the Texas League's entrants actually within the state's boundaries, and this arrangement remains today. Of the league's original entrants in 1888, only San Antonio still fields a team, its status as the nation's seventh-largest city certainly qualifying it for a higher standing than Double-A baseball. Still, San Antonio's more than one hundred Texas League seasons make the Missions the stalwart of Texas League clubs, with league offices located within the city. But few remember that it was the small cities of North Texas that helped place San Antonio on the baseball map over a century ago, paving the way for one of the longest-running minor-league franchises in one of the nation's oldest professional baseball circuits.

While the cities, teams and season results make up most of the recorded history of the early Texas League's franchises, the true stories of this forgotten era remain buried in the census records, family histories, obituaries and newspapers of the day. While some players, owners and executives are remembered for their accomplishments in baseball, few experienced any sort of fame beyond their normally brief careers in the public eye. Most simply returned to a rural life or moved to the city to take a variety of jobs. Some became outlaws or humanitarians. Others met untimely and sometimes violent deaths. But the individuals noted below played, managed, operated a franchise or served as an executive or outside influence, at least for a time, in one of the small cities helping to build the Texas League.

Rick Adams's thirteen-year professional career, including appearances at the major-league level, was followed by retirement as a farmer in Paris, Texas. He was most proud of striking out Ty Cobb in one of his major-league appearances and loaning Tris Speaker his uniform so that he could play his first game with Cleburne in 1906.

Paris native and Major Leaguer Rick Adams is buried in Providence Cemetery near his hometown. *Karen Rutherford photo.*

Bert Adrian was an accomplished skeet shooter and telephone repairman, once falling fifty feet from atop a pole and suffering only bruises.

Roy Akin played fourteen years of professional baseball and achieved the remarkable feat of both fielding and hitting into unassisted triple plays over the course of his career. Akin also discovered an abandoned baby while on a road trip in Seattle, later adopting the child and eventually retiring as a cotton buyer.

Archibald P. Bailey left baseball and became a jewelry manufacturer. He remained active in sports, operating a fishing camp and dying on a golf course in 1937.

Having once pitched a no-hitter and slammed four home runs in a single game, Clyde Bateman was a well-known troublemaker who was eventually stabbed by a good friend during a dispute in Milwaukee. Barely surviving, Bateman refused to press charges and spent his post-retirement career as a night watchman.

Walter "Heavy" Blair.
Author's collection.

Former college football player and 1897 Paris Midland Warren Wallace Beckwith eventually joined the U.S. Army, but he first married the granddaughter of Abraham Lincoln despite her family's objections. Prior to their eventual divorce, he fathered the last living direct descendant of America's sixteenth president.

Walter "Heavy" Blair appeared in 442 major-league games before eventually retiring as an insurance salesman.

George Bristow was a World War I veteran with the First Arkansas Infantry.

William Bulger became involved in the horse racing business and entered local politics in El Paso.

Brownie Chamberlain, who played five minor-league seasons, was an amateur matador who crossed the border on occasion to participate in bull-fighting exhibitions in Mexico.

Zena Clayton served as a scout for the Brooklyn Dodgers and became one of the first players to successfully sue a major-league team when the St. Louis Browns were ordered to reimburse him for unpaid wages.

Telegraph operator and minor-league umpire Oliver Conn was killed when he slipped into the path of an oncoming streetcar in Decatur, Illinois, in 1903.

Pearce "No Use" Chiles, wanted for rape during the 1896 season, was eventually sentenced to prison for participating in a con game. He escaped and is thought to have eventually played professional baseball in the Pacific Northwest.

Jay "Nig" Clarke, who hit eight home runs in Corsicana's historic victory over Texarkana, became a welder's helper and died on the forty-seventh anniversary of his record-breaking feat.

Ed Clark was wounded in the Spanish-American War and eventually taken prisoner by the British when he joined the Boer rebellion in South Africa. He later became a bartender and is buried in Arlington National Cemetery.

J.P. Crearer, owner of the Sherman-Denison Interurban Railroad, served in Belgium and France with the Canadian army in World War I and later became an accomplished tennis player and golfer.

Jay "Nig" Clarke. *Author's collection.*

Gus Creely followed a brief major-league career as a housepainter in Missouri.

Statistically, Dode Criss beat Ty Cobb for the 1908 American League batting title but was disqualified for too few at-bats. Later, Cobb noted that had Criss not played in the Deadball Era, he would have gone down as one of baseball's most feared hitters.

Elmer Countryman was charged with embezzling $600,000 from a bank in Illinois in 1921. While awaiting arraignment in the courtroom, he pulled a revolver from his pocket and committed suicide.

After his career, Don Curtis became a scout and is credited with discovering Hall of Famer Dizzy Dean.

Charles Jerome Dewitt died of tuberculosis just two years after pitching Texarkana's 51–3 loss to Corsicana in 1902.

Walter "Hickory" Dickson played five major-league seasons before dying of the flu in 1918.

Billy Doyle became a scout and is credited with discovering three Hall of Famers: George Sisler, Branch Rickey and Hank Greenberg.

Following his experience as a baseball owner in Temple, John Ewing Edens returned to the Navarro County ranching business, allowing Texas A&M University to use his property to develop new farming and ranching techniques.

1902 Paris franchise owner Charles Eisenfelder later served as president of the Charleston franchise of the South Atlantic League and eventually returned to Galveston, where he managed real estate.

Gus Fisher, a major leaguer for two seasons, was known to answer requests for autographs by signing "Here is my name" on slips of paper.

J.W. Gardner owned the Dallas Texas League ball club for fourteen years and later operated the Gardner Ice Palace, where he introduced Texans to ice hockey.

Ned Garvin posted a 58-97 major-league record and is considered by many to be the unluckiest pitcher in major-league history, as he received little run support during the course of his career. The notorious drinker was suspected but not charged in several violent crimes and eventually died of tuberculosis at the age of thirty-four.

Max Gibbs fought in the Third Texas Infantry of the Spanish-American War and later became a bricklayer.

George Gilpatrick owned a laundry service in Kansas City and died of a fall in 1941.

Edward Howland Robinson (E.H.R.) Green lived lavishly off his mother's estate until he died in 1936. He was buried in Bellows Falls, Vermont, alongside his leg, which had been amputated when he was a teenager.

Before managing a beer parlor in Austin, Hunter Hill, his father and his brother were charged with murdering a farm tenant over crop payments. They were acquitted.

Bert Hise served as Brown County sheriff in the 1920s and received a commendation from the NAACP for helping prevent the lynching of a black prisoner.

Argus Hamilton was known as the "pitching parson," refusing to play baseball on Sundays and eventually becoming a full-time Methodist minister.

Texas League founder John McCloskey once knocked Mikey "Sky High" Hobright unconscious during a game for insubordination. Hobright went on to become institutionalized.

Tom Huddleston became county commissioner of Bell County and oversaw construction of the county's road system.

A.C. Jantzen played in 1,500 games and went on to become a tailor. He was the uncle of longtime professional ballplayer Heinie Jantzen.

Jack Jarvis was heavily involved in horse racing and invented the mechanical starting grid, still in use in horse racing today.

George Kahlkoff played twenty minor-league seasons with eighteen teams, retiring as a sheet metal worker in Louisville, Kentucky.

William Louden managed in the Blue Ridge League and later owned a garage in West Virginia.

Irishman Con Lucid played for several major-league teams but is best known for the remarkable accomplishment of winning thirty games in thirty days in the Pacific Northwest League. He also passed on signing Honus Wagner to a contract, saying that Wagner was "too awkward" to be a successful batter. Lucid later committed suicide.

Harry Maag was born to Swiss parents and later worked in an Ohio rubber factory.

Wilson Matthews was a longtime Texas League umpire and is represented in the Texas League Hall of Fame. He is credited with introducing Ty Cobb to several major-league scouts.

Reeve McKay played with Milwaukee of the American Association and retired as a Dallas firefighter.

Tom Menefee was known to sport a wild western appearance on the ball field and possessed a yell that "would have done credit to a Comanche brave."

William Miller, 1904 Paris co-owner, moved to New York City and continued his career as a typesetter.

Pitcher Roy Mitchell was a member of the 1919 World Series champion Cincinnati Reds, who defeated the infamous Chicago Black Sox. Though a member of the pitching staff, Mitchell did not appear in the Series.

One of the most popular sportsmen of the twentieth century, Uncle Charlie Moran was a college football player, major leaguer and longtime major-league umpire. He also coached eighteen years of college football, posting a 121-35-1 record with four universities. In 1921, he coached Centre College to a victory over Harvard in what has been called the greatest college football upset of the twentieth century.

Roy Mitchell. *Author's collection.*

This modest gravestone near his Tom Bean, Texas home marks the grave of legendary Texas Leaguer Cy Mulkey. *Karen Rutherford photo.*

Henry Byron Mock, promoter of the 1906 Greenville franchise, became a Vermont lawyer and served as a delegate to Woodrow Wilson in the Baltimore Democratic Convention.

John Morris served five years as Texas League president and was instrumental in the development of fourteen minor leagues nationwide.

Cy Mulkey continued a long career in the Texas League as an umpire, eventually retiring to his hometown of Tom Bean to manage a cotton gin.

William "Kid" Nance played twenty-one minor-league seasons, appearing in over 1,500 games, and later managed a number of minor-league teams.

Sandy Neville, secretary of the Paris franchise, continued as a newspaper editor until his death in 1956.

One-time Paris team president Augustine O'Neill remained in the cotton business and served three terms as a Paris alderman.

Paris's Jim Patrick served as legal counsel for the Lone Star Baseball League prior to his death in 1927.

Dudley Payne retired from baseball at an early age and became a dentist.

Isaac Pendleton changed his last name three times during his lifetime, eventually becoming a grocery clerk and bill collector.

Future postman Walter Pease committed eighty-five errors in ninety-seven games in 1901.

Hugh Perry helped organize Grayson County baseball before continuing in the book business, eventually founding the Texas School Book Depository in Dallas.

Dee Poindexter followed an eight-season minor-league career as a cotton compress manager in three Texas cities.

Player-manager Frank Quigg followed his baseball career by obtaining his law license in Kansas. On New Year's Eve 1909, he was part of a gang that attempted to rob a bank in Harrah, Oklahoma. Immediately upon dismounting his horse, Quigg was shot dead by marshals who had received a tip about the pending robbery.

John Raley retired from baseball in 1914 and became a West Virginia coal miner.

Guy S. Rall, co-owner of the 1904 Paris franchise, retired as a furniture salesman in Houston.

Branch Rickey played only three seasons of minor-league baseball but went on to become one of the sport's most beloved and respected figures when he signed Jackie Robinson to play for the Brooklyn Dodgers and integrated baseball in 1947. A World War I veteran, he was inducted into the National Baseball Hall of Fame in 1967.

Roxy Roach played four major-league seasons, fathered fourteen children and became well known as an inventor of unique flies used in trout fishing, as well as an operator of a pool hall, bowling alley and Ford dealership in Michigan.

Left: Longtime major leaguer Harry Steinfeldt's career was inadvertently jump-started by Texas Leaguer Russ Steinhoff. *Author's collection.*

Below: Tris Speaker's grave in his hometown of Hubbard. *Karen Rutherford photo.*

Doak Roberts served as president of the Texas League until his death in 1929.

William Salmburger played fourteen minor-league seasons and managed three seasons in Wichita Falls before becoming a traveling salesman.

Ben Shelton retired to Terrell and remained in the cotton business until his death in 1945.

Russ Steinhoff unwittingly launched the career of longtime major leaguer Harry Steinfeldt when Galveston mistakenly protected Steinhoff rather than Steinfeldt in the off-season. Detroit quickly grabbed Steinfeldt, who went on to play in over 1,600 major-league games.

Tris Speaker went on to a Hall of Fame major-league career, largely with the Boston Red Sox, and is considered by many to be among the greatest outfielders to ever play the game.

Wirt Spencer managed the Texas A&M University baseball team and went on to become a top Texas League umpire.

Sam Stovall followed his seven-season career as a dairy driver in Kansas City.

Harry Tackaberry, heir to the Famous Fort Worth saddle maker, followed his brief Texas League career as a railroad engineer and bartender before being killed in an argument over his wife in 1903.

Rube Taylor pitched one major-league season in 1903 before being killed by a streetcar in Dallas in 1905. The streetcar operator stated that it appeared to have been a suicide.

Jake Thielmann played seven major-league seasons, was a World War I veteran and suffered a beating at the hands of John McCloskey during a game. McCloskey, though, felt sorry for Thielmann and took him to the hospital, after which Thielmann called McCloskey a kind man.

Frank Valdois played thirteen minor-league seasons before becoming a candy maker and chauffer.

Neal Vance had a chance at the major leagues in 1908 but was released after attempting to shoot a teammate during an argument. He later became a chemist with a Tulsa oil company and was found dead in his hotel room from carbon monoxide poisoning in 1919.

Foley White. *Author's collection.*

After a three-season baseball career, William Van Dresser became an illustrator in New York, designing covers for Jack London novels and reaching fame as a well-known artist.

Harry Vitter ended his career in 1907 before becoming a waiter.

Dr. Robert R. Walker left Paris for Oklahoma City, where he became president of the Oklahoma City Mets in the Western Association.

W.H. Ward spent his later years saddened at what he perceived as lack of public interest in minor-league baseball, dying just a year after helping to rejuvenate the Fort Worth Cats.

Pete Weckbecker, accused during his career of stealing gate receipts and leaving players unpaid, was a Spanish-American War veteran and is buried in Hampton National Cemetery.

Robert Westlake played seventeen minor-league seasons with twenty teams, retiring as a West Virginia farmer.

Roland Wolfe was noted as a good ballplayer but "shy in the brain works," largely due to his hobby as an amateur boxer.

Foley White was a World War I veteran who later served as a firefighter in Dallas.

George "Lucky" Whiteman played in a one-time minor-league record 3,282 games over twenty-four seasons, including a still-standing record of 1,132 Texas League games.

William "Lucky" Wright served as an umpire and railroad switchman.

After a nine-year minor-league career, Bill Yoke became a hotel manager in Washington State.

Bill Zeis was blacklisted by the Western Association for unknown reasons but was a known pickpocket.

BIBLIOGRAPHY

Newspapers and Periodicals

Arkansas Gazette
Austin Statesman
Commerce Journal
Daily Oklahoman
Dallas Morning News
Denison Herald Democrat
Fort Worth Star-Telegram
Galveston Daily News
Greenville Herald Banner
Paris News
San Antonio Express
Sherman Register
Sporting Life
Sporting News
Temple Daily Telegram

WEBSITES

Ancestry.com
BaseballAlmanac.com
Baseball-Reference.com
FindaGrave.com
The Handbook of Texas Online (http://www.tshaonline.org/handbook/online)
NewsBank.com
NewspaperArchive.com
The Portal to Texas History (http://texashistory.unt.edu/)
The Society for American Baseball Research (http://sabr.org)
TexasGenWeb (http://texashistory.unt.edu/)

BOOKS

Ashby, Linda. *Images of America: Sherman*. Charleston, SC: Arcadia Publishing, 2011.

Benoit, Patricia K. *Historic Temple: An Illustrated History*. San Antonio, TX: Historical Publishing Network, 2009.

Borneman, Walter R. *Rival Rails: The Race to Build America's Greatest Transcontinental Railroad*. New York: Random House, 2010.

Coppedge, Clay. *Texas Baseball: A Lone Star Diamond History from Town Teams to the Big Leagues*. Charleston, SC: The History Press, 2012.

Falls, Judy, and Sylvia Wood. *Images of America: Delta County*. Charleston, SC: Arcadia Press, 2011.

Grammer, Timothy G., and Jim Bell. *Images of America: Paris*. Charleston, SC: Arcadia Press, 2011.

Grayson County, Texas Genealogical Society. *Ancestors and Descendants: Grayson County, Texas*. Sherman: Grayson County, Texas Genealogical Society, 1980.

Hankins, Bill, ed. *A Pictorial History of Lamar County and the Red River Valley*. Marceline, MO: D-Books Publishing, 1996.

Hunt, Donna Hord, and Mavis Anne Bryant. *Images of America: Denison*. Charleston, SC: Arcadia Publishing, 2011.

Johnson, Lloyd, and Miles Wolfe. *Encyclopedia of Minor League Baseball*. 3rd ed. Durham, NC: Baseball America Inc., 2007.

Kayser, Tom, and David King. *The Texas League's Greatest Hits: Baseball in the Lone Star State*. San Antonio, TX: Trinity Press, 2005.

Kayser, Tom, and Scott Hanzelka. *The Texas League of Baseball Clubs 2013 Media Guide and Record Book*. San Antonio: Texas League, 2013.

Kirsch, George B. *Baseball in Blue and Gray: The National Pastime During the Civil War*. Princeton, NJ: Princeton University Press, 2003.

Masterson, V.V. *The Katy Railroad and the Last Frontier*. Norman: University of Oklahoma Press, 1978.

McElroy, Sherrie S. *Black Land, Red River: A Pictorial History of Grayson County, Texas*. Virginia Beach, VA: Downing Company, 1993.

McGraw, Jack Frost. *Tracks of Time: Remembering the Interurban and Wood Lake*. Sherman, TX: Big Barn Books, 2004.

McGuire, Jack, and Robert S. Stevens. *Katy's Baby: The Story of Denison, Texas*. Mount Pleasant, TX: Nortex Press, 1991.

Neville, Alexander White, and Skipper Steely. *Backward Glances*. Volumes 1–2. Paris, TX: Wright Press, 1983.

O'Neal, Bill. *The Texas League, 1888–1987: A Century of Baseball*. Austin, TX: Eakin Press, 1987.

Piner, H.L. *Sherman's Black Friday: A History of the Great Sherman Tornado*. Sherman, TX: Register Printing House, 1896.

Ruggles, William. *The History of the Texas League of Professional Baseball Clubs*. Dallas: Texas Baseball League, 1932.

Rutherford, Kris. *Homeseekers, Parasites, and the Texas Midland: The Texas League in Paris, 1896–1904*. Maumelle, AR: RecWatch Publishing, 2009.

Seymour, Harold. *Baseball: The Early Years*. Oxford, UK: Oxford University Press, 1989.

Stringer, Tommy. *Images of America: Corsicana*. Charleston, SC: Arcadia Press, 2011.

Walker, Mike. *Comprehensive Railroad Atlas of North America: Texas*. UK: Steam Powered Video Publications, 2001.

Whitten, D. Wiley, Jr. *Champions of Naught Six: The Story of the 1906 Cleburne Railroaders*. N.p.: self-published, 2010.

Wright, Marshall D. *The Texas League in Baseball: 1888–1958*. Jefferson, NC: McFarland and Co., 2004.

INDEX

I

J

K

L

M

N

O

P

Q

R

S

T

W

Z

ABOUT THE AUTHOR

Kris Rutherford is a part-time Lamar County, Texas resident who has been researching the early Texas League for nearly a decade. He is the author of *Homeseekers, Parasites, and the Texas Midland: The Texas League in Paris, 1896–1904*. Kris has been involved in youth sports for over thirty years and has written the middle-grade sports novels *Batting Ninth* and *Nothin' But Net*. He has also been published in several parks and recreation trade magazines. Kris makes his permanent home in Maumelle, Arkansas. In his spare time, he enjoys studying sports history, watching sports, traveling and exploring old cemeteries.